Race, Gender, and Leadership in Nonprofit Organizations

Also by Marybeth Gasman

Marybeth Gasman, Valerie Lundy Wagner, Tafaya Ransom, and Nelson Bowman, *Unearthing Promise and Potential: Our Nation's Historically Black Colleges and Universities* (2010)

Marybeth Gasman (Ed.), *The History of Higher Education: Methods for Uncovering the Past* (2010)

Marybeth Gasman and Christopher Tudico (Eds.), *New Essays on Black Colleges: Triumphs, Troubles, and Taboos* (2009)

Marybeth Gasman, Benjamin Baez, and Caroline Turner (Eds.), *Understanding Minority Serving Institutions* (2008)

Andrea Walton and **Marybeth Gasman** (Eds.), *Philanthropy, Fundraising, and Volunteerism in Higher Education* (2008)

Marybeth Gasman, *Envisioning Black Colleges: A History of the United Negro College Fund* (2007)

Alice Ginsberg and **Marybeth Gasman** (Eds.), *Gender and Philanthropy: New Perspectives on Funding, Collaboration, and Assessment* (2007)

Marybeth Gasman and Katherine V. Sedgwick (Eds.), *Uplifting a People: Essays on African American Philanthropy and Education* (2005)

Patrick Gilpin and **Marybeth Gasman**, *Charles S. Johnson: Leadership behind the Veil in the Age of Jim Crow* (2003)

Marybeth Gasman and Sibby Anderson-Thompkins, *Fund-Raising from Black College Alumni: Successful Strategies for Supporting Alma Mater* (2003)

Also by Noah D. Drezner

Noah D. Drezner, *Philanthropy and Fundraising in American Higher Education* (2011)

Race, Gender, and Leadership in Nonprofit Organizations

Marybeth Gasman, Noah D. Drezner, Edward Epstein,
Tyrone Freeman, and Vida L. Avery

Foreword by Charles R. Stephens

palgrave
macmillan

RACE, GENDER, AND LEADERSHIP IN NONPROFIT ORGANIZATIONS
Copyright © Marybeth Gasman, Noah D. Drezner, Edward Epstein,
Tyrone Freeman, and Vida L. Avery, 2011.

First published in 2011 by
PALGRAVE MACMILLAN®
in the United States—a division of St. Martin's Press LLC,
175 Fifth Avenue, New York, NY 10010.

Where this book is distributed in the UK, Europe and the rest of the World,
this is by Palgrave Macmillan, a division of Macmillan Publishers Limited,
registered in England, company number 785998, of Houndmills,
Basingstoke, Hampshire RG21 6XS.

Palgrave Macmillan is the global academic imprint of the above
companies and has companies and representatives throughout the world.

Palgrave® and Macmillan® are registered trademarks in the United
States, the United Kingdom, Europe and other countries.

ISBN: 978–0–230–12039–6

Library of Congress Cataloging-in-Publication Data

Race, gender, and leadership in nonprofit organizations / Marybeth
    Gasman . . . [et al.].
       p.   cm.
    ISBN 978–0–230–12039–6 (hardback)
    1. Nonprofit organizations—United States—Management.
    2. African Americans—Charities.   3. Women in charitable
    work—United States.   4. Women philanthropists—United
    States.   I. Gasman, Marybeth.
    HD62.6.R33 2011
    658'.048—dc23   2011018675

A catalogue record of the book is available from the British Library.

Design by Integra Software Services

First edition: November 2011

10 9 8 7 6 5 4 3 2 1

Printed in the United States of America.

This book is dedicated to those who bring us laughter, comfort, and inspiration.

Contents

Foreword

Some years ago, as a member of the faculty of a well-regarded fundraising training program, I was assigned to conduct a training session for senior students at an Oklahoma seminary. The choice to send me to deliver the training was made, I am sure, solely because I was then chief development officer at one of the nation's largest theological centers. When I arrived and met my contact, it was clear that the fact that I was a person of color had not been communicated.

By the time of the first break, all anxieties had been relieved and the training program was progressing nicely. My host, in all candor, indicated that he did not know "my people" were engaged in this work, this work of philanthropic fundraising, advancing America's tradition of giving and sharing. When he was told that this had been, at that time, a 20-plus year career for me (now 50-plus), he was absolutely amazed. Sad to say, this attitude about people of color and philanthropy continues even until today.

Typically, in the minds of the majority population, philanthropy is practiced, primarily, by the majority. People of color and other minorities, primarily, are the recipients of philanthropy. The assumption is that majority-defined philanthropy (giving that benefits unknown others) is the only philanthropic practice that matters. The attitude is that "our people" are not on board with that concept yet and are not likely to be at any time in the foreseeable future even though examples to the contrary are all around us. Clinging to this misconception has resulted in philanthropy by people of color being characterized in terms such as mutual benefit, faith-based focus, community-based bootstrap assistance, and social and civic club benefits. When a person of color makes a gift to an institution external to his or her community, the action is highlighted in media outlets as a significant departure from the norm.

This attitude toward philanthropy among people of color has also contributed to the lack of interest among scholars in studying and documenting philanthropy by people of color. Why would one be motivated to study something that does not exist? And certainly if people of color are not philanthropic, why would anyone deign to hire them to manage philanthropically-focused institutions? Further, why would programs in philanthropic studies seek out people of color to engage as students in their programs? So the lie feeds on itself and becomes a self-fulfilling prophesy.

Then along comes *Race, Gender, and Leadership in Nonprofit Organizations*, which speaks eloquently to the achievements of several outstanding individuals whose life circumstances lay waste to the misconceptions about people of color and philanthropy. It is important to note that the examples here are but a few of the hundreds who have persevered against enormous obstacles to achieve in a field that has been tremendously unwelcoming. This book, seriously read and reviewed and integrated into philanthropic studies classrooms, will help to de-sensitize the negative environment impeding the inclusion and advancement of racial and ethnic minorities and women in America's philanthropic enterprise.

For its continuing credibility around the world as a nation where philanthropy and diversity are foundational elements to ultimate democracy, America needs to internalize the seminal lessons about philanthropic endeavor by people of color and women imparted by *Race, Gender, and Leadership in Nonprofit Organizations.*

Charles R. Stephens
Former Chair,
International Association of Fundraising Professionals

Acknowledgments

A few years ago, I was asked to be on the board of Third Millennium, an initiative dedicated to increasing knowledge about philanthropy in communities of color and among youth populations. At one of the initiative's meetings, the board members were told about an oral history project that was being conducted as part of the Third Millennium work. Female and African American leaders were being interviewed about their experiences working for nonprofits and foundations in the United States. As someone who has written books on both African American philanthropy and gender and philanthropy, I asked how the interviews would be used. After a short discussion, I offered to produce a book based on the interviews—and this book is the result of those efforts.

Pulling this book together was an endeavor that took the contributions of many individuals. First, I'd like to thank Larry Smith, the director of the Third Millennium Initiative, and his staff. Likewise, I am grateful to the Indiana University Center on Philanthropy for once again supporting my work and trusting me to conduct research under the auspices of the center. I would like to thank the W. K. Kellogg Foundation for funding the Third Millennium Initiative and this project, in particular. I am also grateful to Angela Logan, who conducted the oral history interviews that were used in this book and Dwight Burlingame and Tim Fischer for their guidance throughout the research, planning, and writing process.

Several of my research assistants at the University of Pennsylvania helped me on this project, including Tafaya

Ransom, who compiled the supplementary bibliography, and Darryl Peterkin, who helped me to conceptualize the book's organization. I was also supported throughout the writing process by my research assistants Valerie Lundy Wagner, Julie Vultaggio, April Herring, Esther Ra, and Thai Nguyen. In addition, my colleagues at Penn provide a supportive work environment in which it is easy to thrive personally and professionally. Often there are others who offer support in meaningful ways, although they are not directly connected to a research program. I am grateful to Nelson Bowman for his friendship and advice while I was writing this book. I thank my sweet daughter Chloe, who is always the inspiration for all that I do. I will always remember this book, in particular, because there was a huge snow storm in Philadelphia and Chloe begged me to stop writing and go out and play.

Lastly, I wish to thank my coauthors on this book project. Noah Drezner and Vida L. Avery are both my former Ph.D. advisees. They have made me immensely proud. Both have accomplished so much in a short time and remain my good friends. Tyrone Freeman is my mentee. He sought me out and asked if I would serve in this role, and of course, I obliged. Tyrone is pursuing a Ph.D. at an institution other than my own. Oftentimes, people ask me why I work with so many young people around the country, and for me the answer is that it's a way to give back—a way of paying forward the success I have had in my own career thus far. I can't wait to see the future success Tyrone will have. And Edward Epstein has been a constant source of inspiration and support to me for the past 20 years. He is by far the most intelligent and compassionate person I have ever encountered in life.

Marybeth Gasman

I cannot truly write the words to thank my father, David Drezner, for the love, confidence, and support that he has given me throughout my life. His love for me is clear in all of his actions and has been a source of strength and encouragement. My mother,

Linda Drezner, of blessed memory, although we only had ten years together, is the one person who inspired my passion for and the study of philanthropy—both monetary and service—most.

While my nuclear family is small, I am blessed with an extended family that is always there for support—a special thank you to my Aunt Judy and Uncle Steve Lippard, my cousins Alex, Josh, and Sandra Lippard; Irene and Donald Greenhall and Audrey Greenhall and George Chressanthis. Beyond my family, over the past few years, I have been privileged to have had wonderful friendships that morphed into familial relationships—those type of connections where you would do anything for them and they likely would do the same for you. These extended families have given me not only support, strength, and abundant happiness over the years but also the chance to engage, be inspired by, and play with a number of children. I am continually amazed and motivated by all of the children in my life. They are sweet, loving, intelligent, and innocent—the kind of innocence that pushes me to strive for the world that they see through their eyes—one in which social justice and civil rights are commonplace. Thank you in particular to Chloe Epstein, Philip, Matthew and Christopher Baldridge, and my little cousins Emily and William Chressanthis along with Lucy and Annie Lippard for continuing to make me believe.

Without the support and friendship of them and their parents, I am not sure where I would be. In particular, I wish to thank Marybeth Gasman, Edward Epstein, and Alan Baldridge, who welcomed me into their families and lives as if I was always there. I look at the strength of our relationship and feel as if you are the siblings that I never had. I thank each of you for allowing me to confide in you and having the opportunity to learn from your wisdom.

Additional appreciation must go to Marybeth Gasman. Marybeth has kindled a passion within me to formulate an active research agenda, while having a love for the classroom, and a dedication to students. Marybeth's commitment to her scholarship and to her teaching has inspired me to develop a teaching and research philosophy that is shaped by a commitment to civic responsibility. She is simply a mentor on whom I will always model myself.

Noah D. Drezner

I am thankful to Marybeth for nurturing my career in research and writing, and for providing comic relief. My daughter Chloe always inspires me to do good work. Lastly, I am grateful to all those on the board and staff of the University City Arts League who gave me a new perspective on nonprofit leadership and board governance. I will carry those lessons with me wherever I go.

Edward Epstein

I thank God for his many blessings. I thank my beautiful wife, Michelle, for her love and support throughout this endeavor and every day of my life since we met at Lincoln University (PA) as freshmen years ago. To my children, Alexander and Olivia, I love you and thank you for loving me unconditionally. Always follow your dreams! To my parents, Rev. William and Carolyn Freeman, thank you for giving me a love of learning. I thank the best sibling in the world, my dear sister, Lanniece Hall; Union Baptist Church of Orange, New Jersey; and all of my family in New Jersey, Delaware, Pennsylvania, Illinois, Maryland, Virginia, and North Carolina. Throughout my academic career, I have been blessed with strong, supportive mentors who encouraged my writing, so I'd like to thank LuElla Peniston, Sheila Foor, Linda Keys, Lilya Wagner, and Andrea Walton. I also thank Dwight Burlingame, Les Lenkowsky, the Philanthropic Studies faculty, Angela Logan and my colleagues at the Center on Philanthropy at Indiana University. To my wonderful coauthors, it has been a privilege sharing this experience with you. Finally, I want to thank Marybeth Gasman, who befriended me as an awestruck doctoral student three years ago at a conference and has supported me to no end ever since. An inspiration and a friend, she is truly a model mentor and a testament to the power of—what I call—teaching as philanthropy.

Tyrone Freeman

I would like to thank Marybeth Gasman for providing this opportunity and encouraging me to get back to what I love: research and scholarly writing. I am most grateful for her unyielding confidence in my abilities and for her love of the field of philanthropy that led to her being my dissertation chairperson. I would also like to thank my parents, Dr. and Mrs. Parnell Avery, for their unwavering support and encouragement with all of my endeavors. Additionally, I am grateful to my sister, Sibyl Avery Jackson, for understanding the plight that writers and scholars go through when starting from scratch, churning an idea around in their heads, and finally laying it down on paper. Michael Bieze has always been my collegiate soul mate and lent a helpful ear when I needed it. And lastly, I am thankful to Pat Smith for editing my rough drafts and allowing me to talk through my ideas, even though at times they were confusing even for me.

Vida L. Avery

Introduction

Race and gender, but especially race, are still subjects that are hard to address, even in social change organizations.
—The Annie E. Casey Foundation, 2005[1]

As we write, global economic turmoil is affecting the foundation and nonprofit world in a way that it has not for some time. Such instability is bound to occur, and bound to recur, as the world of philanthropy is not immune to business cycles. But as we have found in doing our research, issues of diversity, inclusion, and organizational effectiveness present an ongoing and more vexing problem, regardless of the economic situation. Women and people of color are increasingly dominating communities in the United States in terms of numbers; yet the staffing of the philanthropic and nonprofit arenas does not reflect the communities these entities serve. Because of the demographic shift within the past few years, the U.S. Census Bureau now identifies some states as "majority-minority."[2] Because of this change, most spectrums of the nonprofit arena are focusing attention on diversity and inclusion, from reviewing and developing grant-making policies to analyzing the racial composition of the staff, CEOs, and trustees in order for these organizations to run more effectively.

Research on philanthropy among women and African Americans has grown over the past ten years with the publication of several major studies. Marybeth Gasman and Katherine V. Sedgwick edited *Uplifting a People: Essays on African American Philanthropy and Education* in 2005, which focused on myriad forms of philanthropy within Black communities, both in history and in the current day. However, this research pertained mainly to African American philanthropists and not the Blacks serving in leadership positions at nonprofits.[3] In 2007, Alice Ginsberg and Marybeth Gasman edited a volume titled *Gender and Educational Philanthropy: New Perspectives on Funding, Collaboration, and Assessment.* Although this book looked closely at gender issues, the subject matter was strictly grant making. The authors detailed the work of certain leaders of nonprofits and talked about the way that their gender influenced their grant-making activity as well as the importance of using a gender lens when distributing grants.[4] Bradford Smith, Sylvia Shue, Jennifer Lisa Vest, and Joseph Villareal authored a book titled *Philanthropy in Communities of Color,* which focused on philanthropic behavior in Black, Latino, Asian, and Native American communities. The authors worked to dispel the myth that philanthropy is only an act of the wealthy. They argued that ethnic philanthropy is defined by people of modest means sharing with people they know well. The book hints at ways to secure philanthropic contributions from these communities but does not delve into the leadership of the philanthropies with which they are involved.[5]

Janice Gow Petty wrote *Diversity in Fund Raising,* which also focuses on philanthropy in communities of color and offers strategies for fundraising within these communities. Again, however, no attention is paid to leadership within the nonprofits that seek to raise funds from these communities of color.[6] Mary Ellen Capek and Molly Mead, in their book *Effective Philanthropy: Organizational Success through Deep Diversity and Gender Equality,* recommend strategies to nonprofits that want to strengthen their commitment and dedication to diversity and gender equity. Capek and Mead, though, do not cover the lives and experiences of nonprofit leaders.[7] Lastly, Sondra Shaw and Martha Taylor authored *Reinventing Fundraising: Realizing the Potential of Women's Philanthropy,* which pertained to women as philanthropists.[8] Like the Gasman and Sedgwick book, this one offers a new perspective on philanthropists but does not center on leaders within the nonprofit setting.

In addition to these scholarly and practitioner-focused books, numerous studies have been conducted on foundations' and nonprofits' internal structures and staff compositions, forums convened for diversity dialogues, and coalitions formed to place diversity on the philanthropic sectors' agenda.[9] For example, a 2008 survey published jointly by CompassPoint Nonprofit Services, the Annie E. Casey Foundation, the Meyer Foundation, and Idealist.org and titled "Ready to Lead?" describes in detail the challenges facing the rising generation of nonprofit leaders.[10] What is missing from this research is a close examination of the experiences of current female and African American employees in high-level positions with foundations and nonprofits—those who can provide insight into the cultural and life experiences they bring into leadership positions.

Additionally, in 1999, the Council on Foundations published "Cultures of Caring: Philanthropy in Diverse American Communities." This report examined potential ways to expand the use of institutional philanthropy in four population groups: African Americans, Asian Americans, Latinos, and Native Americans. The report aimed to expand institutional philanthropy within these communities. It used interviews of affluent donors from these racial and ethnic communities, as well as fundraisers, foundation staff and board members, tribal leaders, church leaders, and scholars, to understand how these communities view philanthropy in their own cultural context.[11]

Our book centers on the lives and experiences of this group of foundation and nonprofit leaders. We have examined race and gender as constructs and provided a theoretical background for understanding their effect on the psychosocial development of the individuals. We explore their family backgrounds and childhood experiences as well as the impact of education on their lives and future leadership. We also delve into more personal topics and probe the influence of religion and spirituality on the leaders' decision making and disposition toward philanthropic work. We illuminate the leaders' personal perspective on their multifaceted development and experiences. Much like any leader, these individuals faced challenges in their careers and have made personal sacrifices to dedicate their lives to doing work in the third sector. We explore these challenges and sacrifices throughout the book.

The book is organized into seven chapters, besides this introduction. Chapter 1 provides short biographies of each of the leaders who were interviewed for the book. The next chapter delves deeply into the constructs of race and gender and looks at the influence of these factors on the leaders' lives and careers. Chapter 3 examines the leaders' background and family influences. Here we explore the impact of parents, role models, and home environments as well as the effect of historical events and movements on the lives of the leaders. In Chapter 4, we examine the leaders' experiences in primary and secondary school as well as higher education. Chapter 5 examines the effect that religion and spirituality had on these leaders' lives. Belief has had a unique and abiding role in the culture of various minority groups and in the movements that brought about emancipation and equality. At the same time, a profound tension has existed between traditional religious culture and the push toward gender equality. In Chapter 6, we draw upon the voices of the leaders to delve into the challenges and difficulties that they have faced in their roles and in their ascension to leadership. And the last chapter provides a conclusion that brings together the main themes and ideas in the book. We end the book with a supplementary bibliography to aid future scholars in addressing research related to philanthropic and nonprofit leaders.

CHAPTER 1

The Leaders

The findings of this book are drawn from the writings and teachings of nonprofit and foundation leaders. In order to understand these leaders' perspectives, it is necessary to be familiar with their lives and careers. This chapter presents a short biography of each of these leaders. As part of the Third Millennium Initiative, the Center on Philanthropy at Indiana University chose to interview these leaders within a larger effort to understand diversity in fundraising and the nonprofit sector. In order to be considered for participation, leaders had to hold, or to have previously held, the title of "vice president," "executive director," "president," "program officer," "trustee," or another similar title at a 501(c)3 (religious, educational, charitable, scientific, literary, testing for public safety, etc.) or 509(a)1 (a sub-section of those nonprofits deemed as publicly supported charities) organization. The interviews were conducted using a questionnaire adapted from that used by Ella Edmondson and Stella Nkomo for their study *Our Separate Ways: Black and White Women and the Struggle for Professional Identity*[1], which examined African American and White female executives' professional identity formation in the private sector.

Denise McGregor Armbrister. Armbrister is a Black woman of West Indian descent and is senior vice president and executive director of the Wachovia (now Wells Fargo) Foundation. She came to this position with extensive banking and nonprofit experience. Since 1984, Armbrister has worked at Wachovia in commercial banking and has specialized in healthcare, education, and government banking. Her most recent position at Wachovia before joining the foundation was vice president and manager of government underwriting and portfolio management for the Northeast region. She began her career in commercial banking at Chemical Bank (Chase) in New York. Armbrister also served for three years as chief of staff for the president of the University of Pennsylvania. She has been a board member of Harcum College, the Achievement Foundation, Inc., the Delaware Valley Grantmakers Association, and the Forum of Executive Women and a life member of the National Black MBA Association. In 2007 she was appointed to the Philadelphia School Reform Commission by Governor Edward G. Rendell. Her awards and honors include the 2001 "Salute to Women of Achievement Award" by the March of Dimes, a 2003 citation as one of the "Best 50 Women in Business" in the Commonwealth of Pennsylvania, and the 2005 "Women of Distinction" award of the *Philadelphia Business Journal.* She holds a bachelor's degree in mathematics and psychology from Wellesley College and an MBA in finance and marketing from the University of Chicago's Graduate School of Business.

Heather Arnet. Arnet is a White female and executive director of the Women and Girls Foundation of Southwest Pennsylvania. She is also a member of the school board of the Pittsburgh Public Schools, the regional vice president of the Pennsylvania Women's Campaign Fund, a board member of Grantmakers of Western Pennsylvania, and an advisory board member of the Forbes Funds. She serves on the Education Committee of Western Pennsylvania's Planned Parenthood and is an active member of the National Organization for Women, the Women's Funding Network, and Women in Philanthropy. In addition to her activism and philanthropic work, Arnet writes and directs feminist theater. Most recently, she received a grant from the Pennsylvania Council on the Arts for her play *Yo' Mama!* Arnet has spearheaded the Women and Girls Foundation's efforts to pursue legislation at the city, county, and state levels to achieve the foundation's stated goal of fair representation for women on Pennsylvania's appointed boards, authorities, and commissions. In 2005, Arnet and Women and Girls Foundation led a group of young women from the Allegheny County Girls as Grantmakers on a "Girlcott" of the clothing store Abercrombie & Fitch for selling T-shirts bearing sexist messages. The campaign was featured nationally on NBC's *The Today Show*, and the "Girlcott" forced the company to pull the shirts out of stores. Arnet earned her BA from Carnegie Mellon University in literary and cultural studies and drama.

Karen Kelley Ariwoola. An African American female, Ariwoola has been vice president of community philanthropy at the Minneapolis Foundation since 2002. She is affiliated with the Association of Black Foundation Executives and is a strong advocate for mentoring among minority philanthropy leaders. She grew up in Galesburg, Illinois, and earned her undergraduate degree in early childhood education from Western Illinois University and her master's degree in family studies from DePaul University. She began her career in Chicago and then moved to Minneapolis, where she started working with the Minneapolis Foundation in 1994. She currently serves on a number of nonprofit boards, including that of the Minnesota Council of Foundations, where she is vice chair.

Dwayne Ashley. Ashley is African American and past president and CEO of the Thurgood Marshall College Fund (TMCF) in New York City. TMCF provides scholarships, endowment-building assistance, and education and employment programs to public historically Black colleges and universities. Under his agency, the TMCF has built relationships with the Coca-Cola Company, Miller Brewing, ING, Microsoft, Hewlett Packard, and Gallup. Previously he has worked as a regional director in the Philadelphia office of the United Negro College Fund and as the national executive director for 100 Black Men. Ashley was born in Houston, Texas, and is a graduate of historically Black

Wiley College and of the University of Pennsylvania's Fels School of Government. He serves as a historic preservation commissioner for the City of Newark and a board member of a library just outside of Newark.

Susan Taylor Batten. An African American woman, Batten joined the Association of Black Foundation Executives as president and CEO in January 2009. Previously, she was senior associate with the Annie E. Casey Foundation in Baltimore, Maryland. At Casey, Batten served in the Community Change Initiatives Unit, which helped to develop and transform neighborhoods. She also worked to address racial disparities in the foundation's grant making. Prior to Casey, she served as vice president at the Center for Assessment and Policy Development. She also worked with the U.S. Department of Agriculture's Food and Nutrition Service and for several years for the government of the District of Columbia on comprehensive children's initiatives. In particular, she concentrated on efforts to coordinate early childhood programs and policies across the city. Batten is a member of Hispanics in Philanthropy, serves as an advisory board member to the Diversity in Philanthropy Project, and co-chairs the Steering Committee for the Partnership for Prince George's County, Maryland. She studied at two historically Black institutions, receiving her bachelor of arts degree in English and political science from Fisk University and her masters of social work degree from Howard University.

Caprice Bragg. An African American woman, Bragg is vice president for gift planning and donor relations at the Cleveland Foundation. Previously, she served as the Cleveland Foundation's director of planned giving and before that as a gift planning officer. Prior to joining the Foundation, Bragg practiced law at KeyCorp and at Benesch, Friedlander, Coplan & Aronoff LLP. She also was an employee benefits and human resources consultant with Ernst & Young LLP. Bragg serves on the State of Ohio's Commission on Cultural Facilities; the Cleveland

Metropolitan Bar Association's Estate Planning, Probate and Trust Law Section Committee; and Lake Ridge Academy's board of directors. She is also active with the Estate Planning Council of Cleveland (past president), In Counsel with Women, and AdNet, an organization for development professionals in community foundations. Bragg is a board member for the Black Professional Association's Charitable Foundation. The Akron native graduated with honors from Oberlin College with a bachelor's degree in government and earned her JD degree from the New York University School of Law.

Willis K. Bright Jr. Bright is an African American who has served as director of youth programs at the Lilly Endowment since 1996. Previously he was manager of issues and research at Honeywell's Corporate and Community Responsibility Department. He has also served as a faculty member at the University of Minnesota. Bright began his career in social services, directing an urban ministry program and working as a youth specialist for the Iowa 4-H and Youth Services. He is also a founding member of the Black Family Development Consortium. He hails from Lexington, Kentucky, and served in the military as a captain in the Medical Service Corps. Bright earned his undergraduate degree at the University of Kentucky and his master's of social work at the University of Michigan.

Nancy Burd. A White woman, Burd is vice president for grant making at the Philadelphia Foundation. Previously, she was the founding director of Philadelphia's Nonprofit Finance Fund, which provides loans and grants to Philadelphia-area nonprofits. At the Finance Fund, she advised nonprofits in a range of areas, including community development, capacity building, leadership development, and nonprofit finance and management. Burd has been a featured speaker at the Yale School of Management Philanthropy Conference, Harvard Business School's Social Enterprise Initiative, the University of Pennsylvania's Wharton School of Business, and Fels Institute of Government. She is an adjunct professor at the Fels Institute, where she teaches nonprofit and foundation management. She has also authored or coauthored several papers on general operating support and capacity building and led studies on arts policy and development. Burd holds a master's degree from the University of Pennsylvania.

Emmett D. Carson. Carson is African American and a native of Chicago. He is the founding CEO and president of the Silicon Valley Community Foundation. Before coming to Silicon Valley in 2006, Carson served as president and CEO of the Minneapolis Foundation for 12 years. He has authored more than 100 works on philanthropy and social justice. He served as the first manager of the Ford Foundation's worldwide grant-making program on philanthropy and the nonprofit sector. His seminal work on African American giving and volunteering at the Joint Center for Political and Economic Studies is widely seen as helping to spark broad public interest in ethnic philanthropy studies. In addition to serving on numerous nonprofit boards, including chair of the Council on Foundations, he has conducted workshops on endowment building for nongovernmental organizations in southern Africa. He has received numerous awards, including honorary degrees from Indiana University, Morehouse College, and the National Hispanic University. Carson received both his master's and PhD degrees in public and international affairs from Princeton University and his bachelor's degree in economics, graduating Phi Beta Kappa from Morehouse College.

Lauren Y. Casteel. An African American woman, Casteel is vice president of philanthropic partnerships for the Denver Foundation. Previously, she was president of the Hunt Alternatives Fund in Denver, which focuses on areas such as women's and children's rights, and social justice. She was executive director at the Temple Hoyne Buell Foundation in Denver, where she focused on helping families and children. Born in Omaha, Nebraska, Casteel lived in Atlanta, Georgia, Cambridge, Massachusetts, and New Rochelle, New York, as a child. She attended Swarthmore College and earned a degree in communications from the University of Colorado, Denver. Casteel has traveled widely and, in particular, was influenced by a trip to Eastern Europe that took place during the height of the Cold War. Her father was Whitney M. Young Jr., civil rights leader and executive director of the National Urban League.

Lisa Courtice. A White woman, Courtice has been vice president for community resources and grants management at the Columbus Ohio Foundation since 2003. Her responsibilities are to oversee the development and implementation of grant policies, program priorities, and areas of strategic grant making. Prior to joining the Foundation, Courtice held leadership positions at Columbus School for Girls, the Childhood League Center, the Center for New Directions, and the Washington Center for Academic Internships in the District of Columbia. She is involved with several boards and community activities in her region, including the Neighborhood Vision Council for the United Way of Central Ohio, the DonorEdge Learning Community, the Community Health Funders' Collaborative, and the Ohio Wesleyan University board of trustees. Courtice received her BA from Syracuse University, MA from West Virginia University, and PhD from the University of Akron.

Yvette Desrosiers-Alphonse. A woman of Caribbean and Central American descent, Desrosiers-Alphonse was a program officer at the Sunflower Foundation, a Kansas-based institution that focuses on health care. Previously, she worked as a program officer at the Rapides Foundation in central Louisiana, which also focused on bringing quality health care to people in its region. She earned her undergraduate degree in sociology from Boston College and graduate degree in public health from Boston University. After serving in the Peace Corps in Jamaica, Desrosiers-Alphonse worked for the city of Boston and the YWCA, promoting awareness of breast and cervical cancer among minority women. She was born in Los Angeles and has lived in the United States, the Caribbean, and Central America.

Alicia Dixon. An African American woman, Dixon was a program officer for the California Endowment. She holds a bachelor's degree in microbiology from University of California, San Diego, and a master's degree in public health from UCLA. Dixon has a breadth of experience and expertise in the areas of women's health, violence prevention, youth, community development, and environmental health. Since she began at the California Endowment in 2001, Dixon has conducted outreach to community organizations to increase their awareness of funding opportunities. She reviews health-related grant proposals from community-based organizations and helps to develop programs to assist underserved communities. A Long Beach resident, Dixon was a founding member of the Women's Health Council at California's Department of Health Services and is an advisory committee member of the Women's Health Collaborative. She was also recently elected to the Board of Funders Concerned about AIDS.

Kanyere Eaton. Eaton is an African American woman and since 2000 has been executive director of the Sister Fund, which blends faith and women's issues. Prior to coming to the Sister Fund, Eaton directed the social services ministry of the Riverside Church, establishing an updated food pantry, an in-house thrift shop, and a shower and laundry facility for homeless New Yorkers. An ordained minister and trained social worker, she earned a bachelor of science degree from Cornell University, a master of divinity from the Union Theological Seminary, and a master of science in social work from Columbia University. She is currently completing her doctor of ministry degree at San Francisco Theological Seminary. Her contributions as a grant maker and activist were recognized by the Neighborhood Technical Assistance Clinic in 2004, the Women's Funding Network in 2005, the Association of Black Foundation Executives in 2005, and the North Star Fund in 2008.

Carol Goss. An African American woman, Goss is president and CEO of the Skillman Foundation in Detroit. Skillman's mission is to improve the lives of children in Southeast Michigan by strengthening their schools and neighborhoods. Goss joined the Foundation in March 1998 as a senior program officer and was named president and CEO in 2004. She has also worked as a program officer at the Stuart Foundation in San Francisco and as program director at the W. K. Kellogg Foundation in Battle Creek, Michigan. In addition to running the Skillman Foundation, Goss is active with numerous nonprofits and philanthropic organizations, including Grantmakers for Children, Youth, and Families, the Association of Black Foundation Executives, Women in Philanthropy, Detroit Area Grantmakers, and the Wayne County Task Force on Foster Care Youth. Goss hails from Detroit and has a BA in sociology and a master's degree in social work from the University of Michigan in Ann Arbor.

Donna Hall. Hall is a White female and CEO of the Women Donors Network, a philanthropic group that promotes women's and progressive causes. Her undergraduate degree is from Stanford University, and she holds a master's of public health degree from the University of California, Berkeley. Before coming to the Women Donors Network, Hall held positions at the Henry J. Kaiser Family Foundation and the Rockefeller Foundation. During her career, she has focused on economic justice, reproductive rights, education, women's rights in the workplace, and international development. Hall speaks nationally and internationally on women and philanthropy, reproductive justice, women's rights in the workplace, civil society, and international development. She was born in Philadelphia and grew up in southern California.

Erica Hunt. A Black woman of West Indian descent, Hunt is president of the Twenty-First Century Foundation. The development economist Robert Brown created this institution in 1971, with a mission to facilitate strategic and effective giving in Black communities. Hunt was born in New York City and earned her undergraduate degree in literature from San Francisco State University. Before coming to the Twenty-First Century Foundation in 1998, she was a senior program officer with the New World

Foundation. Hunt was also a fellow in the Duke University/ University of Cape Town Center for Leadership and Public Values. She currently serves as a participant in Diversity and Effectiveness in Philanthropy, the International Working Group on Philanthropy for Social Justice and Peace, and Rye Collaborative National Progressive Foundations. Hunt has been affiliated with the New York Regional Association of Grantmakers, the National Center for Black Philanthropy, and the Coalition for New Philanthropy. She has published numerous articles and essays on Black philanthropy and in 2008 was the recipient of Spelman College's award for National Community Service.

Reatha Clark King. An African American woman who hails from Pavo, Georgia, Reatha Clark King is the former president and chair of the General Mills Foundation. She attended historically Black Clark College (now Clark Atlanta University) and the University of Chicago and holds a bachelor of science degree in chemistry and mathematics, a master of science degree in chemistry, a master of business administration degree in finance management, and a PhD in thermo chemistry. Previously, she worked as a research chemist for the National Bureau of Standards. She has held a number of positions at York College in the City University of New York: chemistry professor, associate dean for the division of natural science and mathematics, and associate dean for academic affairs. She also served as president of Metropolitan State University. She was elected chair of the board of trustees of General Mills Foundation in 2002. She has also served on the board of directors of numerous corporations, including ExxonMobil and Wells Fargo. She has been a trustee at Clark Atlanta University and the Congressional Black Caucus Foundation. Additionally, she is a life trustee for the University of Chicago. King is the recipient of numerous awards, including 14 honorary doctorate degrees.

Mindy McWilliams Lewis. Lewis is an African American woman and a recently retired associate director at the Cummins

Foundation, Columbus, Indiana. Born and raised in Memphis, Tennessee, Lewis graduated from Mount Holyoke College with an AB in theater arts and received her master's degree in mass communications from the S. I. Newhouse School of Public Communications at Syracuse University. At Cummins she was director of corporate contributions and associate director of the foundation. Before joining Cummins, she held various other positions in government relations, community relations, and human resources, Lewis worked in the public and nonprofit sectors as press secretary and administrative assistant to former Democratic Congressman Harold Ford from Tennessee, and assistant director of communications for the Washington, DC, Urban League. Her professional focus now is managing the development and growth of the Lewis McWilliams Rollins Hubbard Family Foundation, Inc. In addition to her professional experiences, she serves on several boards at the local, state, and national levels. In her home community, Lewis was the first African American to be elected to the Columbus/Bartholomew County School Board. At the state level, she is an appointee to the Indiana Commission on the Social Status of Black Males. At the national level, she serves on two Washington, DC-based organizations: Impact Strategies/Forum for Youth Investment and Grantmakers for Children, Youth, and Families.

William (Bill) Merritt. An African American male, Bill Merritt has been executive director of the National Black United Fund in Newark, New Jersey, since 1987. His background is in social work. Previously, he served in the New Jersey State Bureau of Children's Services, for the Girl's Center of Essex County, New Jersey, and for the Commission on Mental Health in Washington, DC. Merritt was also active in the National Association of Black Social Workers and a member of the City Council in Newark. He has also been active with the National Council for Black Studies and was on the board of the National Center for Responsible Philanthropy. Merritt is a graduate of North Carolina Central University and Rutgers University, where he earned a master's degree in social work.

Morris W. Price Jr. An African American, Price is national program officer at the Gill Foundation, in Denver, Colorado. He is a member of the Gill Foundation's Movement Building Center, which serves the lesbian, gay, bisexual and transgender (LGBT) community. Previously, he worked at the Daniels Fund, whose primary funding focus is education and educational opportunities for low-income students in Colorado, New Mexico, Utah, and Wyoming. There he was the director of university, college, and community relations. After earning his undergraduate degree in communications from Colorado State University, he worked in higher education, serving in admissions management posts at Wabash College, Montclair State, and DePauw University. In the mid nineties, he returned to Colorado as the University of Denver's director of admissions. Price recently completed a master's degree in nonprofit management at Regis University. His community involvement includes the Mayor's Advisory Commission on Youth, Planned Parenthood of the Rocky Mountains, the GLBT Commission of the City & County of Denver, Urban League of Metro Denver, and Volunteers of America. Price is a founder of the Colorado State University LGBT Alumni Association and former president of the boards of directors of the Denver LGBT Center, Rainbow House Daycare, and Colorado Blacks in Philanthropy.

Jasmine Hall Ratliff. An African American, Ratliff is a program officer for the Robert Wood Johnson Foundation, where she focuses on creating greater access to health care and reversing the obesity epidemic that affects many young people. Previously, Ratliff worked with the Missouri Foundation for Health, where she directed the Women's Health grant program and the development of the Smiles Across Greater Missouri Oral Health program. Within the Women's Health grant program, she helped address violence against women by funding various treatment centers and prevention organizations. She has also been a researcher at the Saint Louis University School of Public Health. Ratliff earned a master of health administration degree from the Saint Louis University School of Public Health and a BA from the

University of Virginia. She is a member of the Emerging Practitioners in Philanthropy, and the Association of Black Foundation Executives.

Joseph L. Smith. Smith is an African American and executive director of the Indianapolis Public Schools Education Foundation. He spent several years in the Air Force and worked as an industrial engineer for the Chrysler Corporation before earning his JD and settling in Indianapolis. Previously, he was chair of the Indiana Parole Board. He has also served as chairperson of the advisory committee for the Youth Philanthropy Mission of Indiana and Treasurer of the Family Education Foundation.

Tracy Souza. A White woman, Souza is the president of the Cummins Foundation in Columbus, Indiana, and is also executive director of corporate social responsibility at this institution. She serves as chair of the Indiana Grantmakers Alliance, Inc., and is a board member at the Columbus Area Chamber of Commerce, the Columbus Regional Hospital, and the Community Education Coalition. She has also served as chair of the Human Rights Commission in Columbus. Souza graduated from Indiana University, Bloomington, with a major in religious studies and minor in ballet.

Phillip Thomas. An African American, Thomas is a senior program officer at the Chicago Community Trust. He also teaches in the Masters of Community Development program at North Park University in Chicago. Before taking his current position at the Chicago Community Trust in 2006, he was a program officer at the Woods Fund of Chicago. He has also served as director of development and public relations at Suburban Job Link Corporation, as director of development at the Creative Arts Foundation, and as a research analyst for Berkeley Planning Associates. Thomas's community involvement includes serving on the boards of directors for Chicago Arts Partnerships in Education; the American Civil Liberties Union, Illinois Chapter; the

National Runaway Switchboard; and the Association of Black Foundation Executives. Thomas received a bachelor of arts in political science from historically Black Morehouse College and a master's in public policy studies from the University of Chicago. He was awarded the Connecting Leaders Fellowship from the Association of Black Foundation Executives in 2005.

CHAPTER 2

Race, Gender, and Identity

According to Gara La Marche, president and chief executive officer of The Atlantic Philanthropies, "racial history and racial identities infuse every aspect of life...no separation of the personal and professional [is possible]."[1] Such is the case, too, with gender: to understand the role of race and gender in the philanthropic and nonprofit world, it is necessary to first clarify what we mean by "race" and "gender." We must also understand the mechanisms by which they work: identity, socialization, culture. This chapter builds a lens through which to view race and gender and attempts to give a way to detect and understand their influence. It then uses this lens to examine data in the interviews and gives an overview of identity in this group of leaders. Later chapters delve into the specifics of how race and gender have affected their work, the culture of the organizations they lead, and their effectiveness in dealing with diverse communities. We will begin with definitions of race and gender and then proceed to some general observations about the role they have had in U.S. society, both historically and recently. We will also review what previous research has said about their impact on the philanthropic and nonprofit world.

This chapter will provide a basis for understanding how race and gender shaped these leaders' psychosocial development. It will use a combined cultural, historical, and psychosocial approach to answer the following three questions: First, how did nonprofit leaders develop awareness of their racial and gender identities?

Second, what was the historical context that existed during their formative years and shaped who they are today? Last, how does the influence of race and gender shape these nonprofit and foundation leaders' life's work?

Definitions

Because "race" and "gender" are social constructs, the terms are hard to define. On the one hand, race has been defined biologically as a group of people with "common ancestry and genetically transmitted physical characteristics" (for example, color of skin, eyes, hair texture, etc.) and captured with terms such as Black or White.[2] However, as Ian F. Haney Lopez points out, this definition negates the fact that there is "no one gene found in all Blacks or all Whites."[3] On the other hand, race has also been defined as a social construction that *labels* individuals in order to perpetuate the ideology of superiority and inferiority, thereby purporting racial domination. However, Michael Omni and Howard Winant argue that race is an "unstable and 'decentered' complex of social meanings constantly being transformed by political struggle."[4] While many of the leaders had different ethnic backgrounds, the majority of them identified themselves as either Black or White. Therefore, the use of the term race herein describes individuals who are Black or White.

While most people use the terms gender and sex synonymously, they are not the same. Gender refers to the social construction of roles, behaviors, and activities that society deems appropriate for men and women. Sex is the physiological characteristic that defines individuals as biologically male or female. However, for the purpose of this book the term gender will incorporate roles and behaviors as well as males and females.[5]

Race: From the Past to the Present

When one thinks of race and gender in American society, the historical issues of oppression, inequity, and marginalization of particular groups of people—African Americans and women—come to mind. This country has made great strides to address injustices by enacting laws that make it unconstitutional to discriminate on the basis of race or gender and that allow individuals once disenfranchised their rights and liberties. Nevertheless, W. E. B. Du Bois's assertion in 1903 that the problem of the twentieth century would be "the problem of the color-line—the relation of darker to the lighter races of men in Asia and Africa, in America and the islands of the sea"—still resonates.[6]

Reviewing the events that took place since Du Bois's assertion and with less than a decade left in the twentieth century, John Hope Franklin categorically stated that "the problem of the twenty-first century" would also be "the problem of the color line." Though Franklin admits that he had no "originality or prescience" for reaching such a conclusion, he maintained that the "problem had not been solved in the twentieth century" and therefore it was "a part of the legacy and burden of the next century." He indicated that it followed a pattern "that the nineteenth century bequeathed to the twentieth century" and that "the eighteenth century handed to its successor."[7]

In 2008, the people of the United States elected their first African American president, Barack Obama. Living to witness such an event was, as Franklin asserts, "one of the most historic, if not the most historic event in America's history." Though it is also indicative, as he describes, of the "willingness and ability" of American society to turn a "significant corridor toward full political equality," the election did not materialize without the issue of race being underscored once again on the national stage.[8] During the presidential campaign, Senator Obama made a speech to address incendiary comments that the minister of his church had made and that had been repeatedly broadcast through different media venues. Because the minister's comments had become a racial issue that was spiraling out of control, Obama felt it necessary to address the comments and his relationship with the minister. In doing so, he discussed not only the legacy of race in America, his racial heritage, and the way such a heritage shaped his ideals, but also the complexity of race as an influence on his candidacy and its impact on society:

> Despite the temptation to view my candidacy through a purely
> racial lens, we won commanding victories in states with some
> of the Whitest populations in the country. In South Carolina,
> where the Confederate flag still flies, we built a coalition of African
> Americans and White Americans.

> This is not to say that race has not been an issue in the campaign.
> At various stages in the campaign, some commentators deemed
> me either "too Black" or "not Black enough." We saw racial ten-
> sions bubble to the surface during the week before the South
> Carolina primary. The press has scoured every exit poll for the
> latest evidence of racial polarization, not just in terms of White
> and Black, but Black and brown.[9]

In no other presidential campaign had it been necessary for a
candidate to address race on both a personal and national level.
However, most people believed that Senator Obama received such
different treatment because of his race and thus his speech was
necessary for two reasons. One, Obama is a Black man, and as
such is held to a different standard, and presented a challenge
to the status quo. Two, some people in American society wanted
to maintain the status quo by not allowing anyone, other than
White males, the opportunity to run for the position of the President of the United States. The experience of then Senator Obama
in his bid for the presidency is not unique but an indication of
the overall problem of race and leadership in the United States.
In fact, Black leaders in any capacity cannot ignore the different
ways that others view their leadership.

Gender: From the Past to the Present

Just as the twentieth century opened with the problem of the
color line, in Du Bois's words, so too were there problems regarding women. Women lacked equality, were disenfranchised, and
were afforded personal definition only within the confines of
male domination. Gloria Steinem asserted that patriarchy and
racial divisions shaped our society and limited individuals' success and mobility. She held that a three-part paradigm of dualism

between masculinity and femininity, linear thinking, and the hierarchy of the male-headed household was the instrument that kept individuals locked in a particular status in life, especially women.[10]

Though women have struggled for decades for equality, their labor bore more fruit in January 2009. With his first piece of legislation, President Obama signed the Lilly Ledbetter Fair Pay Act, ensuring that companies pay the same for the same job regardless of gender, race, or age.[11] More recently, in *The Shriver Report,* California's Former First Lady and member of the Kennedy family, Maria Shriver, revealed how women have made great strides when she reported that "half of all U.S. workers are women, and mothers are the primary breadwinners or co-breadwinners in nearly two-thirds of American families."[12]

Despite these accomplishments, the 2008 U.S. Presidential Primaries bore witness to the fact that women still face limitations and that the influence of gender weighs more heavily on women than on men in leadership positions. Evidence of this assertion is revealed with the media's treatment of Senator (now, Secretary of State) Hillary Rodham Clinton. The media's focus on her emotional responses (or lack thereof) on the campaign trail, its targeting of her femininity, and its scrutiny of her hair and wardrobe are all confirmations that America's society has yet to transcend its gender biases in leadership positions, especially those positions that have been dominated solely by men.

As one can surmise, the quandary of the color line, the influence of race and gender on high-profile leaders, and the pattern of maintaining the status quo, especially by passing leadership positions from one White male to the next, still profoundly affect the fabric of American society. The example given above not only pertains to the political arena, but also permeates other leadership positions within America's society, particularly in the philanthropic and nonprofit fields.

Today, foundation and nonprofit leaders are not only publicly addressing the preferential treatment that White males receive in acquiring leadership positions, but also bringing to the forefront the issues of diversity and inclusiveness within the sector. In 2008,

Gara La Marche, president and CEO of The Atlantic Philanthropies, began a speech that he made on race and philanthropy by illustrating racial consciousness and awareness of the systematic advantages he received as a White male:

> What gives me the right to make a speech about race? Well, first off, I have a race. That might seem obvious, but we are so inured to Whiteness as the default position, deeply internalized by virtually all White people and even many people of color, that race is something that only Black and Latino and Asian and Native American people are thought to have. So yes, I am White, and more specifically a White man who by virtue of that carries with him a set of privileges of which finding it easier to hail a taxi going uptown or walk alone on a dimly-lit street at night without fear of being sexually assaulted are just the beginning.[13]

Additionally, La Marche provides insight into what exclusionary hiring practices exist in the third sector and how privilege sets White men apart from all others in gaining access. He added:

> At least in the critical earlier stages of my career, whatever my individual merits, I got taken more seriously because I was a White man, certainly by the White men who had a virtual monopoly on selection and hiring, and I competed in admission and employment pools that were woefully lacking in the available talent of women and people of color . . .
>
> . . . I didn't set it up this way, or even recognize it at the time, and the world has changed a bit—though hardly enough—since. But candor compels me to say that I wouldn't be standing here today, in all likelihood, with a hand on the tiller of nearly $4 billion in philanthropic resources, if I wasn't to some extent the beneficiary of a system of racial privilege and exclusion.[14]

Similarly, other foundation and nonprofit leaders have addressed the exclusionary practices within the nonprofit arena and have brought the necessity for diversity and inclusivity to the forefront. As Emmett D. Carson, CEO and president of the Silicon Valley Community Foundation, explained, for decades "the field of philanthropy had been a bastion of elite privilege, the closed world of institutionalized charitable giving," but now "new forms of wealth are challenging traditional philanthropic practices."[15]

The challenge to which Carson referred is creating a diverse staff that is reflective of the diverse community it serves. "The staff and boards of philanthropy institutions," Carson argued, "have not kept pace with the general population in terms of diversity" and the "statistics on representation in the field haven't changed significantly over the years."[16] La Marche echoed this sentiment when he explained that the current pressure on philanthropy was "to demonstrate its responsiveness to the communities it serves." He warned that if other leaders in the field have "blinders on about race," none of them would effectively meet the goals of their organization's mission.[17] Carson's and La Marche's view of philanthropies and race relations is concomitant to the White House view. President Obama has ushered in more dialogue on race; his administration is also calling for equity, accountability, and transparency within all sectors of society, including nonprofits and foundations.

What remains to be seen is whether this urgency about diversifying nonprofit staffs leads to the cultivation of a rising generation of women and African Americans. Current research shows that many barriers exist to leadership for all groups. The above-mentioned "Ready to Lead?" study by the Annie E. Casey Foundation, for example, speaks of long hours and inadequate pay as putting a damper on the ambitions of many in the nonprofit world. Among minority employees in particular, however, there was a sense that the organizations for which they work do not welcome their advance. Considerably more minorities than Whites believed that they would have to leave their current workplace in order to move up (60% vs. 53%). These statistics are in line with Carson's and La Marche's observations and pose a formidable impediment to diversity. Our respondents provided insight into how they have faced and overcome such challenges.[18]

In *Effective Philanthropy*, Mary Ellen S. Capek and Molly Mead indicated that the most important findings from their research "are the links between foundation effectiveness and institutionalizing nuanced understandings of diversity, including gender."[19]

They argued that when nonprofits discuss diversity, more often than not, the discussions surround only race and class. Having a focus solely on race and class apart from gender presents a "false dichotomy" in that "women and girls are a part of every racial and ethnic group from the most privileged to the least." A more nuanced understanding of "deep diversity" would enable the sector to be more effective.[20]

Most people want to believe they go through their daily lives performing their life's work looking through an objective lens; however, this is seldom the case. There are a number of factors that not only influence individuals' identities, but also shape the lens from which they view the world.[21] The next few sections examine the influence of race and gender on nonprofit leaders by applying a cultural, historical, and psychosocial framework. Subsequent chapters will utilize the framework established here to delve into this question in great detail.

Living History: Racial and Gender Identity Awareness

"To engage in a serious discussion of race in America," as Cornell West posited, "we must begin not with the problems of Black people but with the flaws of American society—flaws rooted in historical inequalities and longstanding cultural stereotypes."[22] The issue of race and gender has always been emblematic of a painful, and at times shameful, history in American society that stigmatized groups of people as second-class citizens, if it acknowledged them as citizens at all. Even though we have legally remedied these issues with respect to citizenship, their lingering effects are still intensely felt emotionally, psychologically, and socially.

In the remaining pages of this chapter, we will develop a framework for understanding the responses of the nonprofit and foundation leaders who participated in this study. The framework will approach the responses on two levels. First, it will view the leaders' development as individuals by taking into account both their formal and informal education. Second, it will focus specifically on the development of their race and/or gender identity. Kenneth Cushner, Averil McClelland, and Philip Safford, in the book *Human Diversity in Education: An Integrative Approach,* named three stages of socialization: "1) primary socialization, socialization of infants and young children by families and other early caregivers; 2) secondary socialization, the neighborhood, religious affiliation, the peer group, the school, as well as mass media; and 3) adult socialization, the socialization of adults into roles, settings, and situations for which they may have been unprepared by primary and secondary socialization."[23] To conceptualize the influence of race and gender on nonprofit and foundation leaders, this chapter intertwines the stages of socialization with historical events that shaped their identities.

In addition to the general socialization stages that Cushner et al. provided, we used the psychosocial framework that William Cross Jr. and Beverly Daniel Tatum developed specifically for racial identity. Cross, a scholar who studies the psychology of African American identity development in the United States, was trained in social-personality psychology. His research focuses on the "theoretical and empirical study of African American identity and personality development across the life span, with particular emphasis on development at and beyond adolescence."[24] Cross named five stages of racial identity development, also known as "psychology of nigrescence" or the "psychology of becoming Black": pre-encounter, encounter, immersion/emersion, internalization, and commitment.[25]

Tatum, a trained clinical psychologist, is an expert on race relations and the development of racial identity. In her book *Why Are All the Black Kids Sitting Together in the Cafeteria?* she used the title as a springboard to a discussion of racial identity and social customs. Tatum incorporated Cross's five stages of racial identity, yet expanded them to include gender by explaining that "just as racial identity unfolds over the life span, so do gender, sexual, and religious identities."[26] Hence, the stages named by Cross will be used in this examination and will include gender as well.

The first two stages, *pre-encounter* and *encounter*, as Tatum explained, are "most prevalent for adolescents." In the first stage, *pre-encounter*, adolescents, both Black and White, are "socialized in an environment that perpetuates the Eurocentric dominant culture [and] presents the stereotypes of superiority and inferiority." Tatum, however, stated that Black parents who are "race-conscious"—those parents who "encourage positive racial identity by providing their children with positive cultural images and messages about what it means to be Black"—lessened the impact of the dominant society's message. At this stage, the "personal and social significance of one's racial group membership has not yet been realized, and racial identity is not yet under examination."[27]

Most of the nonprofit and foundation leaders in our study experienced their primary socialization from their parents or caregivers and went through the pre-encounter stage in the 1950s and 1960s, when American society was struggling with racial and gender equality and democracy. "The struggle for equality in the United States seemed never-ending," as John Hope Franklin asserted. "The United States was quite capable of taking the message of democracy and equality to various parts of the world but was pained beyond description whenever the challenge was confronted at home."[28] Thus, on the one hand, the dominant message and social milieu that these leaders experienced during the pre-encounter stage consisted of a decisive separation of the races. Jim Crow laws enforced *de jure* segregation with the notion of separate but equal on all fronts. Many of these leaders grew up within segregated environments, particularly those who lived in the South; consequently, Blacks were aware of racial differences from birth, as the former General Mills Foundation leader Reatha Clark King illustrated:

> I always had a sense of [being] Black from birth. You know in those days things were segregated, colored and White. If you learned how to go to the toilet on your own, you knew that you ventured into the colored toilets.

While the respondents were socialized from an early age to be aware of difference, they also received positive messages about differences from their families. According to Karen Kelley Ariwoola, vice president of the Minneapolis Foundation,

> My parents talked about race constantly because we were pretty much the only Black kids in our elementary school, the only Black kids in our neighborhood and we went to an integrated church. The fact that we were different was always front and center. My mother is the person who always wanted to take the high road. "Hold your head up high, you come from a great ancestry, you don't have to ever apologize or feel bad that you're Black." We got all those positive messages along with "you have to be better than everyone else."[29]

Even those individuals with multiethnic backgrounds experienced racial and ethnic awareness at a young age. Yvette Desrosiers-Alphonse, program officer with the Sunflower Foundation, had this to say about her identity:

> I was always aware of being a member of an ethnic group. Although my mother is Jamaican and father is Panamanian, because of African descent, I identify myself as Black. In Latin America, you felt because you are Black you are not given opportunities or you're excluded and coming home and [asking] why did the teacher say or do this?

Additionally, parents lessened the impact of stereotypical messages with cultural activities and images, as is demonstrated in what one female leader recalled:

> I was [aware of my racial identity] very early on because my mother was very pro-Black.... I'll never forget it: in elementary school, she was very much [about] African heritage. We were taken to the African Arts Museum and everything. Somehow, I started to enjoy African Folktales and reading them.

On the other hand, the messages and social dynamics consisted of a male-dominated society that limited access and opportunities for females. At the time when many of these leaders were born, society had gender-strict roles for men and women. As Nancy

Burd, vice president for grant-making services at the Philadelphia Foundation, reflected, her mother was "a dynamic woman who was very bright but born at the wrong age." Opportunities were limited "for women [Black or White]; therefore, they had to settle for clerical or administrative work."[30]

Mary Catherine Bateson, a cultural anthropologist and daughter of the renowned anthropologists Margaret Mead and Gregory Bateson, believes that "the issue of inferiority still arises for virtually every woman growing up" in American society.[31] However, women whose parents were gender conscious provided exposure and affirmation within a nonrestrictive environment, as Heather Arnet, executive director of the Women and Girls Foundation of Southwestern Pennsylvania, recalled:

> My mother stressed that you can be whatever you wanted to be. It was very important to her, particularly for me as a young woman; she felt that when she was growing up that that was not a world that was presented to her . . . . She made sure from a very early age that I was given books about female explorers, pilots, astronauts, presidents, and painters.

Arnet further reminisced about the feminist memorabilia she encountered growing up:

> I can't remember a time not knowing . . . not only knowing that I was a female, but that I was a feminist. That was definitely talked about in our household. In fact, one of the first books that I can remember feeling was my own, being around four or five years old, is actually a collection of Wonder Woman comics edited and published by *Ms. Magazine* and the forward is by Gloria Steinem. I mean, it is something that has been a valuable possession of mine since I was very little.[32]

The second stage in racial identity, *encounter,* is "precipitated by an event or series of events that force the young person to acknowledge the personal impact of racism."[33] For respondents who grew up in the Jim Crow south, the encounter was typically with marked indicators of "Colored/Negro" and "White" throughout society and in public places. Several African American leaders attested to racial encounters involving teachers with low expectations; being placed in a lower academic track or being told that certain academic and occupational directions were unattainable. According to Cross and Tatum's theory, adolescents at this stage, "begin questioning what it means to be a member of a group targeted by racism."[34] Joseph L. Smith, executive director of the Indianapolis Public Schools Education Foundation, had his encounter with racism on family trips to the South:

> The most vivid memories were when we'd drive down south and, mind you, Dad would pack, at the time, eight kids in the car and eight bags of chicken, and we would get down past Kentucky and head to Alabama and he would warn us, "Don't drink at the water fountains, don't go to the bathroom in there." I used to always wonder why we stopped along the highway and my sisters would have to get out and if anybody had to urinate, we'd just stop along the roadside and get down beside the car . . . it really wasn't until we got down South when you could feel the fear in my parents about us crossing the line.[35]

Morris W. Price Jr., the national program officer at the Gill Foundation, provides an example of the first time he encountered a young White girl and his awareness of racial tension:

> We were in Fargo, North Dakota and we were in a store. My sister and I were walking down the aisle as little kids, and a White girl came around the corner and she screamed at us because it was the first time that she [had seen] a Black person. And it was the first time we had someone who was White look at us that way. My father said we went back home and we asked, "did we do something wrong?" He had to explain that not everyone felt [the same] about race . . . this was in the early, this was in the mid sixties. That was the first time we became keenly aware that race was an issue and that not everyone was comfortable with us.

One of the most tragic memories of a racial encounter was that of Dwayne Ashley, president of the Thurgood Marshall College Fund. In his words,

> I had an uncle who was killed by the Ku Klux Klan . . . and that
> was my first time seeing the race issue because I didn't really under-
> stand it. That brought it home. My parents had to sit down and
> explain it to me. It was my grandmother's brother. My cousin
> owned a restaurant. . . . They wanted him out of business. There
> was a competing White business in the town. They killed him—
> they shot him. He was sitting down eating in the restaurant and
> he was shot and killed. He was 72 years old. They tried to kill all
> of them but they killed my uncle.[36]

Segregation also existed among the sexes, particularly in employment opportunities for girls and school activities for women.
During the 1950s, employment ads in newspapers were segregated into "Help wanted-women" and "Help wanted-men."
Thus, the announcements themselves disallowed women from
certain fields.[37] Similarly, Heather Arnet provides an example of
how religious sects also segregated the sexes, as demonstrated in
the following exchange:

> I remember saying to one of my favorite Rabbis that I had decided
> that I really wanted to become a Rabbi. He said to me, "You mean
> you want to become a reformed Jew?" which is like the ultimate
> bad. I said, "No, I want to be an Orthodox Jew." He said you
> can't because you are a girl. Either you can become less religious
> or you can stay part of the flock and be the wife of a Rabbi, but
> you definitely cannot be Orthodox and be a Rabbi and be female.
> I was very unsupported.[38]

However, women gained attention during the 1960s with President Kennedy's Commission on the Status of Women, chaired
by former First Lady Eleanor Roosevelt. The Women's Rights
Movement and the rise of feminism were also hailed as influential by the nonprofit and foundation leaders in our study.
Other historical events mentioned were the 1964 Civil Rights
Act and the Voting Rights Act of 1965, which together broke
the last barriers to voting in the South and outlawed formal racial
segregation.

The third stage of racial identity, *immersion,* is when individuals become "very involved with everything related to their race

(for example, characteristics, language, behavior, etc.), a cultural connection, and socializes with individuals within their particular racial [or gender] group, excluding members of other races or genders."[39] According to Emmett D. Carson, when Black people appeared on television during the 1960s, it was an "event in the household" where the entire family gathered around the television and took pride in the race because Blacks were rarely on television shows."[40]

The immersion stage of both Cross's and Tatum's theories corresponds roughly to the secondary stage of Cushner et al.'s socialization construct. In this stage, individuals find safe places of escape "for resisting stereotypes and creating positive identities" and are culturally socialized outside the home.[41] Several African Americans recalled living in segregated neighborhoods, and though this certainly was a result of racism, it nevertheless provided a safe haven from racist messages. Many respondents were also socialized in and identified safe places such as Black churches, Black-oriented social groups, historically Black colleges and universities, and social networks with people of the same race. Whites, incidentally, made no mention of needing such a place.

African Americans, male and female, who went to predominately White institutions of higher education recalled participating in activities or joining groups such as Black student unions, Black Greek Letter Organizations, Black student newspapers, and Black campus forums. A few women chose racial/ethnic housing as a "safe place" on their college campuses in order to connect with others of similar cultural backgrounds. Yvette Desrosiers-Alphonse had this to say about her college experience:

> Boston College had an AHANA house. AHANA stands for African, Hispanic, Native American, and African American. That was truly kind of the pulling point for students of color on campus. It's where you would go for counseling, tutoring and just to hang out. They made sure to try to meet all the students of color and connect that so that you didn't feel like you were this lost soul in this all White campus.

After individuals have totally immersed themselves in their race, they make the transition into the *emersion* stage and socialize more comfortably with others from another race. According to Tatum, an individual at this stage will "unlearn the internalized stereotypes about his or her own group and redefine a positive sense of self" that is "based on an affirmation of one's racial group identity."[42] This is also where Cushner et al.'s schema—adult socialization—begins. The majority of these leaders pursued graduate degrees and hence formed new social circles; some started a family, traveled, or went in the workforce, charting their course into the nonprofit arena.

One might ask how these individuals survived and rose above obstacles to succeed in leadership positions and on a level that few African Americans or women attain. The answer is rather simple, as one female explains; they had to "persevere and do well in spite of." All of these leaders had parents who provided affirmation and fostered the most fundamental kind of esteem: "core" self-esteem.[43] This affirmation enabled them to progress through circumstances and events they witnessed while it also encouraged them to draw strength from their heritage and to rise above and forge ahead.

Impact of Race and Gender on Nonprofit and Foundation Leaders

Many White Americans in particular profess to live in a color-blind and gender-neutral society. On the issue of race, for example, Eduardo Bonilla-Silva has noted that Whites often claim that they "don't see color, just people." Borrowing rather disingenuously from Dr. King, these individuals say they wish to live in a society that judges people "by the content of their character rather than the color of their skin."[44] However, as the Atlantic Philanthropies president La Marche pointed out, such is not the case, especially in the nonprofit world. Every day, the realities of past inequalities impose themselves on the lives of people of color and women in the workplace; how these individuals respond to the different hand they have been dealt has a profound effect on their career trajectories. Therefore, the last two stages of racial and gender identity, *internalization* and *commitment*, are used in this section to demonstrate how the influence of race and gender has shaped nonprofit and foundation leaders.

These last stages, internalization and commitment, pertain to individuals' sense of security about their racial and gender identity. Individuals are willing "to establish meaningful relationships respectful of this new self-definition." Tatum indicated that they "have found ways to translate a personal sense of racial [gender] identity into ongoing action" that expresses "a sense of commitment to the concerns of Blacks [men/women] as a group," as well as become "prepared to perceive and transcend race [gender]."[45] Thus, nonprofit and foundation leaders have translated their sense of racial and gender identity into action. They have become personally committed to racial uplift. As a result of their commitment, these leaders often made themselves instruments of change in the internal culture of their organizations. They initiated discourse regarding race and gender. This is exemplified by comments made by Phillip Thomas, senior development officer at the Chicago Community Trust:

> One of the ways I orient my work is to try to make the organizations I am a part of more responsive to and inclusive of African American communities and all communities of color. I very explicitly and intentionally try to be the voice, and try to represent, not to the exclusion of other groups or a broader view, but I think often that perspective is missing in discussions, and I think that is valued by my colleagues.[46]

Similarly, Mindy McWilliams Lewis, a former associate director at the Cummins Foundation, explained how significant it is to be exposed to diverse perspectives—individuals who have different life experiences—during programmatic decision-making:

> I think [race and gender] had a significant impact because I was able to bring to the table perspectives both from work with the organizations and understanding from life experiences, whether indirectly or directly. Value is added to that organization's focus on issues that impacted people of color and minorities at the table.

I think, also, you have your antenna out there looking at and seeing things differently than other people do and to be able to access
communities and your peers or other folks of color made a difference in terms of the kinds of programs that I was pretty proud
that we were able to support through the foundation.

Regarding gender, women indicated that their experience of being
a woman, wife, and mother made them more attuned to their
female employees' needs of balancing work, family, and children. Being in a position of authority, they had the power to
implement policy changes in response to these needs. Among the
changes they implemented were creating day care centers on-site
that enabled parents to be in close proximity with their children; allowing employees to bring their children to work when
school was closed; establishing flextime, which permitted employees to take care of family needs; allowing employees to work from
home regularly; and creating generous leave policies for men and
women, regardless of sexual orientation. Having such policies in
place, one female CEO explained, produced not only positive
mental health for the staff specifically, but also a positive healthy
environment for the organization as a whole.

Another way these leaders expressed their commitment to
change was by connecting with the community they served. This
could mean conducting research that led to problem solving in
that particular community. Joseph L. Smith, executive director
of the Indianapolis Public Schools Education Foundation, provided this example of why it was important for organizations to
have staff members whose experiences closely mirrored those of
the populations they served:

> When we can stand in front of an audience and talk about our
> experiences, it's more believable. When you talk about having
> been in a march [during] the civil rights struggle...it seems
> to me that passion comes out much more honest, much more
> believable.[47]

For Karen Kelley Ariwoola, diversity worked both ways. Certainly
it meant staff members who could communicate effectively with

the target population. But it also allowed the target population to communicate with the organization—through the staff member who shared their experience and could therefore provide an insider's perspective to the organization's leadership:

> I actually live in the community; my kids go to school in the community. I have a lot of overlapping relationships. I think that adds a lot of value and credibility to the foundation. I've been able to bring a different perspective to the table on a lot of things that [are] respected by my colleagues.[48]

Ensuring that people of color and women had access to the philanthropic profession was another important way that race or gender identity spurred commitment. Conscientious leaders provided career guidance and advice to other professionals from their racial or gender group and encouraged younger people from that group to consider philanthropy as a profession. For example, Susan Taylor Batten, formerly at the Annie E. Casey Foundation, shared how she initiated an outreach to students attending historically Black colleges and universities in her area:

> We pulled the Black colleges together in the area—Howard, Morgan, Coppin, and [Bowie State University]—and talked to a couple of professors and held a seminar on philanthropy as a career option. Students were just blown away and had never even thought about it.[49]

These leaders also actively increased awareness of race and gender issues through different means, such as joining organizations or collaborating with groups that focused on a particular racial or gender issue. In some cases, the respondents formed organizations that had a racial or gender focus for giving.

For example, Phillip Thomas is one of a number of respondents who is a member of the Association of Black Foundation Executives (ABFE), the Council on Foundations' oldest affinity group. As a member, Thomas was instrumental (along with the association) in "convening an informal meeting of foundation staff who were interested in strategizing how philanthropy responded" to the "disturbing trends in levels of unemployment and poor education among African American men and boys." From their actions, "a series of developments in the field of philanthropy helped influence the emergence of Black males as an issue area/demographic to which more funders were paying attention."[50] ABFE produced *Stepping Up and Stepping Out,* which is a report on philanthropic organizations that are making "investments with a specific intent to create opportunities for Black males in their [respective] communities." ABFE anticipated that this and subsequent reports would serve as examples of the steps that philanthropic organizations can take to respond to the crisis affecting Black men.[51]

Female leaders also provided examples of how they fostered awareness of gender and racial issues. Heather Arnet explained how heading the Women and Girls Foundation in Southwestern Pennsylvania and conducting research on women's and girls' issues put her in the position to raise awareness of current gender inequity in the region. Being a well-respected foundation leader, she received plenty of invitations to speak publicly and therefore had many opportunities to inform audiences about the issues facing women and girls. In the same vein, Donna Hall, of the Women Donors Network, led a membership organization of activist women who dispersed at least $25,000 a year to progressive work. Their strategy for giving was to "study an issue from every angle, listen to people most affected, and then engage in activities using a race, class and gender lens." The organization formed different giving circles such as the Election Integrity Action Circle, the Gulf Coast Action Circle, and the Reproduction Rights Action Circle. Such circles are often informal groups of individuals who pool their philanthropic funds to support a common goal.

Lastly, these leaders continued to demonstrate their commitment professionally by leading or working for organizations that reflected their racial or gender identity. Three of the men and four of the women provided examples of this level of commitment. Two of the men are African American and were CEOs of their organizations at the time of the interviews. Dwayne Ashley, for example, was president of the Thurgood Marshall College Fund, which assists students who attend public historically Black colleges and universities. William Merritt is the president and CEO of the National Black United Fund, which works to "provide a viable, systematic, and cost efficient mechanism for Black Americans to make charitable contributions to Black American organizations engaged in social change, development, and human services." A third leader, Morris Price, is a national officer at the Gill Foundation, whose grant-making program promotes gay and lesbian causes.

Similarly, Kanyere Eaton, an African American woman, is the executive director of the Sister Fund, which supports and gives voice to women working for justice from a religious framework. Erica Hunt, also an African American woman, is the president of the Twenty-first Century Foundation, which supports community revitalization, education, and leadership development in the Black community. Donna Hall, a White female, is CEO of the previously mentioned Women Donors Network, which unites women to support of gender-specific causes. Finally, Heather Arnet, mentioned above, leads the Women and Girls Foundation of Southwest Pennsylvania, whose mission is to achieve equity for women and girls in its region.

As this chapter illustrates, the foundation and nonprofit leaders highlighted above developed their race and gender identity during a time of uncertainty and turmoil. Each started life on an unequal level and experienced adversity because of factors beyond his or her control. Each also experienced positive role models, family or community members who instilled in them an appreciation for the positive accomplishments of their race or gender. And so, they disallowed their difference to be an impediment, instead rising above society's expectations. Simultaneously, they saw the social and political fabric that once held the nation's status quo together unravel; they witnessed individuals who had been cast to the margins of society rise up and demand their liberties and equal rights.

All of these leaders experienced discrimination and prejudice on the basis of their race, gender, or sexual orientation throughout their lives, yet turned these experiences into a commitment to race, gender, and sexual minority uplift. Subsequent chapters will examine more closely factors of the environment in which they were raised, conditions in which they were educated, and the problems they experienced later in life as their careers blossomed. Each chapter will build on the thesis developed here: that the leaders' personal development resulted from a pattern of socialization that begins with race or gender consciousness and ends with activism.

CHAPTER 3

Background and Family Influences

There was no question of "if you were going to college," it was "where are
you going to college?"[1]
— Morris W. Price Jr., National Program Officer, Gill Foundation

Although among the respondents to our research there were as
many family situations as there were leaders, common themes
stood out, particularly in the area of education and community.
In this chapter we examine the various background influences that
shaped the lives of these nonprofit leaders. As well as the home
environment, we also examined the historical events that were
important to them and their development. We looked, too, at the
influence of socioeconomic status and family composition. What
kind of expectations did their parents and communities have for
them, and how did these expectations shape their development?
In what ways did their families engage in philanthropic activities
and civic involvement?

The age range of the leaders interviewed for this study is
wide, and as a result their perspective on historical events differs.
The leaders also differ in their race, gender, and socioeconomic
status and in the geography of their birthplace. Yet there were
many similarities in the way they were molded by history, family,
and community. The philanthropic leaders interviewed for this
study all benefited from strong and nurturing home and community environments during their childhoods. Examining their
backgrounds yields insight into the many factors that may have

contributed to their ascension into their current roles as leaders in the foundation and nonprofit world.

Historical Moment

Roughly speaking, the interview respondents can be divided into two groups on the basis of the era in which they were raised. Those born before the civil rights struggles in the United States had direct experience of segregation and its attendant violence. Those born during or after the movement learned about it indirectly, through television or stories told by adults. For the former group, racism was not just a stumbling block but a threat to life and limb; stepping out of one's place could have dire consequences. Although these differing situations did not affect the way respondents chose their careers, they did affect how the interviewees discussed and managed race relations. No similar generational divide existed with regard to gender, because the legal disenfranchisement of women had ceased long ago. However, evolving attitudes about gender—including stereotypes of women's abilities and roles—affected the leaders' attitude toward education and career path.

For leaders of the earlier generation, those born in the 1940s or before, World War II, President Roosevelt's death in 1945, the desegregation of the military in 1948, the Korean War, and the *Brown vs. Board of Education* Supreme Court decision of 1954 were key markers of memory. Of particular pride was the boxer Joe Louis's defeat of the White boxer Billy Conn in 1941.

As noted, for these individuals, history was not a distant occurrence but something they lived through. In Chapter 2 we learned how Reatha Clark King had to use segregated public toilets during the height of Jim Crow in the South,[2] while Joseph L. Smith remembered being warned not to use "Whites Only" water fountains and bathrooms.[3]

Not only was the oppression palpable, but for a number of those interviewed, the forces fighting to change it were as well. For example, Erica Hunt noted that while growing up in Harlem, Malcolm X was not just a figure on television but a fixture in her community: "I saw Malcolm X live in Harlem on the street corner."[4] Such interaction and engagement with the times had a profound impact on her sense of self and justice: "This was a moment to change laws. My whole sense of justice really was formed—I'm talking before the age of ten or eleven . . . People had a right to vote and people had a right to go anywhere they wanted." Susan Taylor Batten reported having a sister who was actively involved with the Black Panther Party.[5] Likewise, Mindy Lewis, who grew up in Memphis, Tennessee, was deeply involved in the Civil Rights Movement, including the events surrounding the death of Martin Luther King Jr.:

> Martin Luther King was eventually assassinated . . . I was right in the middle of all that during my high school experience, so there was clearly some backlash from students and the Black Mondays that we participated in where we didn't go to school on Black Mondays in support of the sanitation workers [whom King came to support just before his death], the strikes, and the civil rights protests that were going on in Memphis at the time.[6]

Being part of the generation of African Americans that witnessed the Civil Rights Movement often meant integrating a school. Several of the older leaders experienced the hardship of being the first of their kind to enroll in a White school during an era of presumed inferiority. For example, Joseph L. Smith was entering third grade when the archbishop decided to end segregated Catholic schools and parishes in Indianapolis:

> We were kind of guinea pigs in 1949. Myself and three of my siblings entered a formerly all White Catholic school. It was very rough on us—I mean very rough . . . the faculty and the kids at school just didn't think that we belonged. And they were just ordinary American citizens. They just didn't think Black folk were equal or should be treated equal.[7]

Most of the leaders interviewed were born during the 1950s or 1960s, while the Civil Rights Movement and the integration process were already under way. When asked which historically significant events stood out in their memories, these leaders frequently mentioned the Cold War, the Civil Rights Movement, and the achievements of African American figures in entertainment and sports. Their memories were charged with the chaos of 1960s and early 1970s—conflicts such as the Bay of Pigs crisis, the Vietnam War, the assassinations of John F. Kennedy in 1963 and Martin Luther King Jr. in 1968, and Watergate. At the tail end of this generation were memories of the Jim Jones cult tragedy in Guyana in 1978 and the Iranian hostage crisis during the Carter administration.

A few of the leaders born in the 1950s and beyond also had a direct experience of the Civil Rights Movement. Carol Goss, CEO of the Skillman Foundation in Detroit, vividly spoke about singing as part of her school choir at a church where King preached prior to his historic march through Detroit, Michigan, in 1963. During this event, he first gave his "I Have a Dream" speech—months before his more famous delivery of the speech during the March on Washington. As Goss recalls,

> Our vocal music teacher arranged to have an ensemble sing at this church where [King] was preaching. [Then we participated] in that march walking down Woodward Avenue where he marched and then gave his speech. That had remained with me always. He was a leader that inspired you to keep going and to keep pushing. We had great confidence in him as a person that he could create the kind of change in our country that would make a difference for all people.[8]

Phillip Thomas recalled the National Guard troops that came through his neighborhood to restore order in the city of Chicago during the 1968 riots that followed King's assassination. He remembered giving cookies at the age of six to a soldier who was stationed on his porch with him, while pondering why the "good guys" (soldiers) were marching through his neighborhood.[9] As an African American, Thomas later recounted the importance of watching the rise of Harold Washington in Chicago politics in the 1970s and 1980s to become the city's first African American mayor; this caused Thomas to think about public service as a career.

For the African American leaders born during the 1950s and 1960s, popular culture, as much as actual events on street, was a touchstone of change in the United States. As well as watching the moon landings, they could tune in to Black actors, who began to appear with some regularity on television. Their presence was not merely about entertainment, but about growing opportunities. Emmett D. Carson, current president and CEO of the Silicon Valley Community Foundation, grew up in Chicago during the 1950s. He noted the important role of Black television shows such as *Julia*, which starred Diane Carroll; *I-Spy*, featuring Bill Cosby; and *Room 222*, which had an African American teacher as a main character. In Carson's words,

> I mean these are shows people don't talk about anymore, but in Black households and in my household, we all watched [them] . . . [they] were just path breaking things, because you didn't see Black people on TV, and that was important in my household to be supportive. Again it wasn't a Black Panther household, but it was a household that took pride in the race. And those were things that my parents would sit back and go "Wow; can you believe it? Things are really changing here." And they made me take note of it that our expectation is that you're going to do things like that. This is the kind of world that's waiting for you.[10]

Clearly, respondents of both the older and younger generations saw a country in the midst of change. But the older African Americans in the group helped to make that change happen. Having borne witness to segregation, they were also on the front lines of civil rights and integration. The younger generation, on the other hand, enjoyed the fruits of civil rights struggle, as exemplified by the more frequent appearance of minorities on television. These advances, however, did not completely erase racial problems.

There is much debate about how much media depictions of minorities changed in the wake of the Civil Rights Movement.

Stephanie Greco Larson has argued that in spite of the wider range of roles available to African Americans, television and film still presented the world from a White point of view. Larson criticizes the shows *I-Spy* and *Julia,* which Emmett Carson mentioned above, for limiting Blacks to a few "acceptable" roles. It was acceptable, for example, to play the "buddy" to a more important White character, as Bill Cosby did in *I-Spy*—and more famously, as Sidney Poitier did in *In the Heat of the Night.* Also fair game was the assimilated main character in *Julia,* a Black nurse who essentially lives in a White world. Either way, television and film reinforced White norms and ignored authentic Black experience.[11]

A more subtle view of contemporary film and television, and one that affirms Emmett Carson's impression of gradual progress, is presented in Jennette Dates and William Barlow's *Split Image.* These authors also acknowledge that post-Civil Rights depictions of minorities on television have mainly served White interests by showing Black life from the White point of view.[12] However, Dates and Barlow also give more credit to the powerful and original performance of these Black film and television innovators, whose efforts represented a critical step forward. Regarding Cosby and Poitier, Dates notes:

> Although some critics argued that the superhero was a reversed stereotype and an unrealistic anachronism, most agreed that the roles played by Poitier and Cosby were a welcome relief from the minstrel characters of early films and television.[13]

The Civil Rights era brought changes in news coverage of minorities as well as fictional depictions. There is widespread agreement that television in particular aided the Civil Rights Movement by generating sympathy for the protesters. Images of Southern law enforcement officers attacking unarmed citizens with dogs and fire hoses, beamed daily into the living rooms of ordinary Americans, tipped the balance of public opinion toward Civil Rights. The print media as well published stories that were generally sympathetic to the movement.[14] Again, Larson challenges this conventional view of history by noting that media coverage of Civil Rights was not all that regular, and many newspapers' editorial staffs (notably the *Chicago Tribune*) were quite hostile to King and his protesters. Positive coverage of civil rights activities presented a White point of view, highlighting the heroic actions of White supporters and ignoring the realities of the lives of Blacks and their reasons for protesting. Moreover, news about Blacks in the 1960s and beyond continued to follow a racist pattern of exclusion or selective coverage. Past media coverage had focused on Black criminality, and similarly there were more stories and images of the rioting in the latter half of the 1960s, according to Larson, than the earlier nonviolent protests. Overall, as the percentage of racial minorities increased in many cities, coverage did not expand proportionately.[15]

It would be fair to say that real shifts in popular portrayals of minorities in both news and entertainment did occur, but these did not signal a complete reversal of racism. The character of the media as an enterprise largely by and for Whites did not change even as toleration of African Americans did. The new racial discourse—in which everyone claimed to be for liberty and justice, but not everyone acknowledged the differing histories of Blacks and Whites—defined the time that the younger generation of leaders matured. As we shall see, this discourse certainly affected the way these leaders responded to problems in the nonprofit and foundation world.

An awareness of social injustice provides an incentive to work at healing the world. Because they have had a different experience of life, members of minority groups are more likely to see the unfair treatment that many people receive in the modern-day world—even when this unfairness is buried in the hubbub of film and television. Perhaps this explains why a greater proportion of young minorities than Whites shows an interest in nonprofit careers. According to the Annie E. Casey Foundation's "Ready to Lead?" study, respondents of color were 10 percent more likely to say "definitely yes" or "probably yes" when asked if they would pursue a leadership role in a nonprofit.[16]

Family Background

Families of respondents in this study tended to be stable. Although the leaders represented a wide variety of socioeconomic backgrounds, parental support was strong in all cases. Some described themselves as middle class or wealthy and others as working class or poor. Over half of the leaders, despite economic status, came from two parent households. Slightly less than one quarter came from divorced households. Two leaders lost a parent during their early years and thus grew up in a single-parent household. One leader grew up in a blended household with a stepfamily. In most cases, the surrounding community acted as a secondary bulwark that reinforced parental involvement. In spite of the discrimination these leaders may have encountered on the outside, in their homes and immediate neighborhoods there was harmony, support, and relative comfort.

Leaders tended to have positive recollections about the communities where they grew up. They often described the communities as "safe" and "carefree."[17] A handful of the respondents spoke of a privileged upbringing. Donna Hall grew up in what she described as a "fancy" all-White community in southern California to parents who were highly educated professionals.[18] Lauren Y. Casteel, now vice president of philanthropic partnerships for the Denver Foundation, was born in the Midwest, but grew up among the Black elite in New York and Atlanta as the daughter of the civil rights leader Whitney M. Young Jr., and she regularly mingled with other families whose members were leading the movement.[19] Lisa Courtice, vice president of the Columbus Foundation in Ohio, reported having a "safe, clean, and affluent" existence in a Washington, DC, community, in which "bad things didn't happen."[20] Tracy Souza, leader of the Cummins Foundation in Columbus, Indiana, described her family's socioeconomic status as "fortunate" but not excessive as a Congressman's daughter growing up in both Columbus and outside of Washington, DC.[21]

A little more than a quarter of the leaders reported growing up in working-class families. Despite the economic struggles of their families, these leaders did not describe a sense of hopelessness. According to Erica Hunt:

> We had no car, we had no yard, and we paid rent. [But] I think the values and aspirations of doing better and becoming something like a teacher or a doctor [were more important]. I marvel at my mom and that whole generation of folks who were able to instill all these values that they really didn't have the economic [ability] to get to themselves.[22]

Another leader remarked about her working-class parents: "I never worried about it at the time growing up. I didn't see it as poor or otherwise . . . they were working class people. We had clothing and food, but we didn't have a lot of extra."[23] While their families definitely struggled to make ends meet, the love, support, and examples of their parents helped create nurturing environments that kept the future philanthropic leaders grounded and safe.[24]

Of the leaders who reported growing up in poor families and neighborhoods, three were born in the pre-civil rights era—one in a Southern segregated community in rural Georgia, one in a working-class community in New Jersey, and the third in the then-segregated Indianapolis. There were a few whose family incomes declined as a result of the loss of a parent. Phillip Thomas described his community as low-income with middle-class values, but his father's death when he was still a baby left his family stuck in poverty despite his mother's heroic efforts.[25] Similarly, Heather Arnet was born in a diverse Miami, Florida community but experienced economic difficulty after divorce forced her mother onto food stamps.[26]

Expectations and Significant Adults

Research shows that expectations of parents have a significant impact on the career aspirations of their children. Mothers are notably influential, especially among young people from rural areas.[27] Without exception, all leaders reported having high parental expectations regarding their education, character, and achievement. Nearly all were expected to do well in school, go to college, and be kind and decent, if not active and engaged, citizens. Yvette Desrosiers-Alphonse, who had several siblings, emphasized her mother's influence: "She made it very clear, very, very clear that the expectation was you were going to finish high [school], you were going to go to college, you were going to get your master's and then after that what you wanted to do was up to you. So all five of us have our master's degrees. My mom doesn't play."[28]

In many cases the parents were well-educated and expected the same of their children. Most of the leaders had at least one parent who had completed either an undergraduate or a graduate/professional degree; one leader's father earned a doctorate. Several of the respondents' parents started college but were unable to finish because of either financial or family obligations. And a few leaders reported having parents with only a high school education or lower. Reatha Clark King, for example, noted that her parents were illiterate, a consequence of their struggle as a sharecropper family in southern Georgia during the Jim Crow era. The town in which they lived, Pavo, Georgia, lacked a formal schoolhouse. Even King's parents, however, expected their children to gain an education. Regardless of the level of education that the parents attained, across the board, these families valued education and held extraordinary aspirations for their children.

Jasmine Hall Ratliff, a program officer at the Missouri Foundation for Health, noted her father's insistence on effort and initiative, when she stated: "He didn't tolerate not trying, particularly academics."[29] Denise McGregor Armbrister, executive director of the Wachovia Regional Foundation, was raised by Jamaican immigrant parents. She remembered her father's admonition to "always learn your lesson."[30] This mantra stayed with her as a reminder not only to do well in school but also to learn from mistakes and life experience. Dwayne Ashley had not only high parental expectations but also the weight of family history thrust upon him. He grew up with family stories about a great-grandmother who was born a slave but still founded a school in the Deep South. So he was also expected to "go on to do great things."[31]

Family expectations were not limited to education but included personal development, character, and employment. Yvette Desrosiers-Alphonse recalled, "[My siblings and I] had an hour of TV and you could decide how you wanted to use that hour . . . Because you only had an hour you ended up doing other things. So we all play a musical instrument . . . cook, do floral arrangement, because you had to do other things. Then we are all voracious readers."[32] Nancy Burd, who grew up in 1950s Philadelphia, spoke of her mother's focus on developing independence in her daughter by encouraging the pursuit of dreams and refusal to settle for "female" jobs.[33] Reatha Clark King spoke of her sharecropper family's insistence that she "be able to get work out of the field and work that would earn more pay."[34]

High expectations in all things were constant regardless of gender, race, geography, or generation. There was, however, an added expectation regarding race. While the White female leaders were encouraged to do well and be happy, many of the African American leaders noted an expectation to be a "credit to the race." According to the sociologist Sarah Willie, it is common for African Americans to bear the responsibility of their race, with many young people feeling that their failure will let down not only their families but their communities and their race as well.[35] Carol Goss provided insight into this "credit to the race" expectation:

> If you didn't live up to it, [Mother] was disappointed, but she made you feel like you were disappointing a whole race of people. That is a whole different way than things happen today because back then you were either a credit to your race or you were not a credit to your race. We had lots of strict expectations around behavior, how you conducted yourself. The rules. That was reinforced around the neighborhood by not only your parents but also others who were always making sure you were on your best behavior.[36]

Even as the families of White women in the study prepared them to address gender barriers, they did not instill in their daughters the additional expectation that their life's accomplishments would reflect on all women. White female leaders did note an imperative not to diminish their career aspirations in order to fit traditional gender roles. The African American women, however, tended to follow a racial rather than a gendered construct. In fact, African American women leaders did not normally discuss expectations—or barriers to success—based strictly on gender. Theirs was still a highly racialized world. The leaders' experiences are quite typical of African American women. According to Johnnetta B. Cole and Beverley Guy-Sheftall in their provocative book *Gender Talk*, "There is perhaps no intracommunity topic about which there has been more contentious debate than the issue of gender relations in Black America. We also believe that the proverbial 'battle for the sexes' has caused deep ruptures in the cohesiveness of African American communities that have not gone unnoticed."[37] As a result, Black women rarely discussed issues of gender. In Patricia Hill Collins' words, "the goal of racial solidarity mandates that Black women remain silent about certain aspects of Black male-female relationships."

Many families found a balance between having what Emmett D. Carson called a racialized household and a nonracialized household.[38] The foundation leader describes being taught by his parents:

> I needed to be twice as good to get half as much...So was it a racialized household? To that extent, yes. But it was also in a curious way a nonracial household, because my mother and father very much believed that the only limit to my success would be my own effort.[39]

According to this way of thinking, a racialized household is conscious of race: it makes known the barriers that our society places on the basis of race—at the same time that it instills a sense of pride in one's race. In contrast, the nonracialized household views individual ability and effort as more important than racial identity. On the one hand, parents wanted their Black children to be proud of their race and to celebrate their achievements and talents through historical examples and current events. These were important countermessages to what Reatha Clark King called "the self-consciousness around being Black...The broader community spoke to you loudly and clearly that you were not to be proud of being Black because that was bad."[40] On the other hand, these parents deliberately sought not to paint a picture of the world as full of limitations based on race. As such, they focused on hard work, education, and initiative as essential for success. We see both of these impulses come together in King, who went on to become a chemist. Describing the forces that shaped her career path, she cited both the historical example of George Washington Carver, about whom she learned through Black History Week activities, and her own hard work and initiative.[41]

The difficulty here was striking the right balance. Failure to acknowledge that the system was unfair—and instead instilling the idea that the only barrier to success was one's own lack of hard work—could lead to a kind of internalized racism. Among the values that Reatha Clark King was taught growing up in the South was "being smart and being willing to work and to work hard, not being lazy. That was a terrible word—lazy." Of course, "lazy" was a common stereotype that White people had about African Americans.[42] Without racial awareness—with only the consciousness that one had to work hard to get ahead—an African American might easily be led to believe that any failures he or she experienced were the result of congenital laziness. The effect that this had on the African Americans in the group—the challenge that it posed to their leadership—is the topic of further discussion in Chapter 6.

The White female philanthropic leaders also needed to develop a consciousness to cope with gender-related barriers. As mentioned earlier, the Women and Girls Foundation leader Heather Arnet recalled that her mother "made sure from a very early age that I was given books about female explorers, pilots, astronauts and presidents and painters."[43] And Tracy Souza's family regularly reinforced the idea that there were "no boundaries based on gender."[44]

These expectations found reinforcement through other significant adults in the early lives of these philanthropic and nonprofit leaders. Many reported having close relations with blood relatives who may have lived nearby or even at a distance. These often included grandparents, aunts, and uncles who took interest in the children, exposed them to new things, and were solid role models. As Carol Goss noted, "We have a very large family. I have a lot of aunts and uncles that I felt very close to. They didn't serve in a parenting role, but they were very much a part of our family."[45] But a far greater number of leaders noted the importance of extended family and fictive kin networks. These were caring adults who may have been godparents, neighbors, the parents of childhood friends, or the close friends of parents, who banded together to provide encouragement, rebuke, and support in the tradition of the proverbial African village raising a child. Much has been said about the role of fictive kin in the lives of African Americans, including their role in philanthropic giving. According to Marybeth Gasman and Katherine V. Sedgwick, in their book *Uplifting a People: African American Philanthropy and Education*, fictive kin are essential to the giving process, with considerable giving taking place to "fictive" cousins, children, aunts, and uncles.[46] This has been found in research examining philanthropic giving across all communities of color.[47] In Lauren Casteel's words, "All of our neighbors in Atlanta had a lot to offer the local children, so they all served almost like parents to us. Everybody helped to raise everybody's children, so everyone was very respectful and working to ensure that the kids in that community grew up with the community values."[48] Of particular note, too, were the immigrant networks of friends that surrounded Denise McGregor Armbrister's family. Her parents sacrificed much to come to the States from the Caribbean and had high expectations and supportive networks of friends to create an environment that enabled her to thrive.

Community leaders and organizations also provided support in these roles. Pastors, teachers, Boy Scout leaders, and other adults were also mentioned as having a significant presence in these third-sector executives' lives. As spiritual leaders, pastors frequently visited their homes and interacted with family members. Teachers, who often lived in their communities, also provided support and encouragement for the children outside the classroom. According to Lauren Y. Casteel, "Everybody has the right to 'call you out' if you are not behaving, so I can think of many adults who were friends of my parents who were around as well as just [in the] neighborhood. They were teachers. They were neighbors."[49] We also observed nonprofit community-based organizations such as the YMCA and after-school programs serving as organizational surrogates for parents and emphasizing expectations for behavior and character.[50] Clearly, philanthropic leaders were nurtured by an array of blood and close relations that created networks of support and care along with boundaries for behavior that aided in their development. Such nurturing offered clear advantages in these leaders' life and career. It provided an impetus for achievement in education and work, as well as the self-confidence to exceed any limitations posed by lingering race and gender discrimination. It may also have given the leaders a consciousness of the ingredients necessary for a better life and hence influenced their career path and the product of their work. Leaders who had reaped the benefits of strong families, good education, and nurturing communities would indeed have an interest in spreading those advantages to others who share their background.

Philanthropic Activities

The concept and importance of philanthropy can be transmitted from one generation to another. Bentley and Nissan found that primary school students learn philanthropy and altruistic behavior by witnessing an influential adult, such as a parent, a teacher, or a religious or youth organization leader engage in acts of prosocial behavior—voluntary acts to support others.[51] Using the 1992 Survey of Giving and Volunteering in the United States, Schervish and Havens found that witnessing at least one parent or guardian perform volunteer work and being the recipient of help while young were associated with higher levels of giving as an adult.[52] The author Morton Hunt referred to this as modeling theory.[53] Others have noted that philanthropic modeling is intensified when it is accompanied by awareness—that is, when the role model discusses the importance of such actions.[54]

During the interviews, most leaders reported some form of community engagement in activities that would be considered philanthropic. The few who reported no engagement noted barriers to participation generated by particular family circumstances such as a divorce or a death that left the family without the time or resources for such activity. But these were exceptions, as most participated in a range of activities both formal and informal.[55]

Interestingly, many did not use the term "philanthropy" in relation to the kinds of activities they participated in or observed their families doing. According to Reatha Clark King, "The word 'philanthropy' just wasn't in the vocabulary. I don't know what we called it specifically but we didn't call it philanthropy."[56] The tendency among African Americans not to use the word "philanthropy" is quite common and has been identified in several research studies. Words such as "sharing" are more common.[57] Joseph L. Smith noted that it "was very clear that you shared what you had . . . that was considered philanthropic. Next door to us, the neighbor grew corn and she would share it with us."[58] This ethic of sharing was prominent among the leaders' families and revealed that two types of voluntary action for the public good took place, one formal through organizations and the other informal through networks.

The many acts of sharing that the leaders spoke of occurred within and between families and members. These acts are categorized as informal or in-kind philanthropy. Much like giving to "fictive kin," informal giving is identified in the literature as common within African American communities and other communities of color.[59] Leaders spoke of cutting the neighbor's grass, caring for the elderly, and generally being available to help others as the kind of activity that sustained their community. Reatha Clark King, for example, recalled sharing basic food items with the neighbors who didn't have enough to eat.[60] People not only shared food staples, but also leveraged other resources. Phillip Thomas recalled that it was common for his mother to drive strangers to church: "it was not unusual for my mother to stop on the street if she saw, an elderly person ... going to church with her hat on or something, and picking her up and taking her to church. Not even our church ... she would drive down the street, and just like stop and pick somebody up and take them to church."[61]

Carol Goss's mother belonged to a group that made "cancer pads" for local hospital patients. Goss mentioned, "I didn't know what those were for. They would get together, and they would make these cancer pads, and they would take them to the hospital ... [Mother] later told me that back then they had patients who had cancer, who spent long hours in the bed. They would have sores, and these pads were used to help with that."[62] And Dwayne Ashley remembered, "[My father] would stop and change [women's] tires and would never accept money. They tried to pay him but he was teaching my brothers and me about giving back."[63]

For some, philanthropy was more involved and made use of particular skills. For example, Susan Taylor Batten recalled how her educator-father created an after-school homework club that he ran out of their basement. He would tutor kids from the neighborhood and plan field trips to expose them to new knowledge.[64] One senior program officer noted that having taken piano lessons as a child, he volunteered to play music for weekly church services. Another philanthropic leader spoke of her father's engagement in a men's group that supported local kids, raised money for college scholarships, and hosted picnics for the neighborhood. She also recalled fondly how her mother's commitment to her profession of social work carried over into their home: "She lived that 24 hours a day. There were always kids in our house. She was always generous."[65]

Many of the leaders who grew up in the 1950s reported involvement in the Civil Rights Movement as a kind of philanthropy. Erica Hunt discussed how family members and neighbors actively raised funds and sent money to support the movement. They also regularly "went on a bus to go and support things."[66] Because of her father's civil rights involvement, Lauren Y. Casteel had an intimate look at the logistics of the movement as strategies were literally planned at the dinner table in her home. As she pointed out, "It was all about the advancement of us as a community and as a people. I never knew differently."[67] Mindy Lewis reported her family's commitment to the Civil Rights Movement through local organizations in Memphis, as she recalled, "I saw firsthand their commitment and desire to be engaged in the Civil Rights Movement so that those liberties, opportunities, and privileges were available to particularly African Americans living in the South. I saw that firsthand and understood that firsthand. I saw my folks put themselves out there on the frontline."[68]

While informal philanthropy was common, many of the leaders interviewed reported more formal giving as well. Among the recipients of such giving were groups such as mutual aid societies, the Urban League, the League of Women Voters, the National Organization of Women, and the Masons.[69] Within the African American community, one of the most important and frequent recipients was the church, to which many families gave a significant portion of their income. Giving to the church will be discussed extensively in Chapter 5.

Whether their giving was formal or informal, families of leaders in this study gave actively. They looked out for family members, neighbors, and friends; they also worked through organizations to serve others and challenge the status quo. There is no question that such examples influenced the leaders' values, career choices, and own philanthropic and community engagement today.

In reviewing the family backgrounds and childhood experiences of the philanthropic and nonprofit leaders in this study, it is apparent that all came from loving families with extraordinarily high expectations for academic performance, personal character and behavior, philanthropic service, and civic engagement. They also tended to be surrounded by supportive communities comprising blood relatives, fictive kin, neighbors, friends, and community leaders who took an interest in them and helped create a community environment that reinforced the values of their homes.

The leaders interviewed for this study experienced a watershed moment in U.S. history. At the time of their upbringing, profound changes were taking place in race relations and gender roles. The older members of the group recalled experiencing the oppression associated with segregation in America and were on the front lines of integration. The historical moment in which they were raised forged their commitment to social justice, education, community development, racial uplift, and gender equality.

Among the most important influences in the early lives of these leaders were parents who stressed the value of education. Without exception, these individuals grew up with a strong commitment to attaining higher education. The next chapter will explore the leaders' education and the impact it had on their later lives and work.

CHAPTER 4

Education

For many of these third-sector leaders, school provided as much of a formative experience as home and community. School was the site of the secondary socialization named by Cushner et al. as one of three stages of identity development. In line with Cross's Tatum's notion of racial identity development, it was also the place where many leaders reported an encounter with racism or immersion in a cultural community related to their race. Just about every possible educational context was represented in the experience of the leaders. They attended public, private, and parochial schools. Some attended segregated schools, and others racially diverse and integrated schools. Parochial school settings included Jewish, Catholic, and Lutheran. And among the more atypical settings were Department of Defense public schools on military bases, a freedom school developed during the civil rights era, and a one-room country church that doubled as the school house for a rural Georgia community. Respondents attended a range of institutions of higher education as well, including state universities, small liberal arts colleges, historically Black colleges and universities, and Ivy League or other highly competitive private universities.

On close examination, the school experiences of the philanthropic and nonprofit leaders reveal much about their character development, interests, and later career trajectories. Their co-curricular activities and relationships with teachers and guidance counselors provide insight into their personal and academic development. In particular, it is clear that early opportunities for leadership made a difference in their long-term career interests. We will see that support from educators and educational institutions was uneven, but as noted in the previous chapter, encouragement from family members was strong and consistent.

Leadership and Engagement

At the secondary school level, leadership in student activities was common among this cohort of third-sector leaders. Nine held roles in student government, including student council president and vice president of the senior class. This includes an African American woman who became student council president in a predominantly White high school in 1960s Ohio as well as a president of the Black student union in 1970s Virginia. Given the fact that the United States was just emerging from a period of *de facto* and legalized segregation, these individuals demonstrated immense bravery taking on these roles. Gill Foundation officer Morris W. Price Jr., who grew up as a military child and was educated at Department of Defense schools, noted that "student government was big in our house. Leadership was really big in our house."[1] Along with student government, seven leaders reported involvement in athletics such as tennis, track, dance, basketball, volleyball, flag corps, and football.

In addition to student government and athletics, there were other kinds of co-curricular engagement. Seven respondents reported involvement with the arts, including music, choir, band, orchestra, drama/theater, and radio. Ten leaders reported involvement in scholastically oriented clubs and organizations, such as the Latin club, honor societies, science club, Spanish club, French club, journalism, yearbook, history club, Model United Nations, and the debate club. Others reported involvement in service-based groups such as the Boy Scouts, Key Club, and Jack and Jill.

There were also some unique co-curricular activities that demonstrated the creativity, academic talent, and leadership potential of the study's participants. One respondent attended a school that awarded points for involvement, so she and a friend created their own club that would allow them to avoid sports, which they did not like, and engage the arts, about which they were passionate. Their club, titled Relief from Boredom, presented concerts and other cultural events for the school community.[2] Another leader was selected as a Congressional Page and spent time working for the federal government in Washington, DC.

It was rarely the case that the leaders did not participate in some form of co-curricular activity. Clearly, both participation and leadership were valued. These activities not only helped the future executives develop their talent and abilities, but also kept them out of trouble. As one respondent put it, "I grew up under the theory that busy is better."[3]

The Importance of Teachers

Relationships with teachers were critical, particularly for the African Americans interviewed. Teachers not only formally educated the leaders in terms of school curriculum but they also provided support and encouragement for pursuing higher education. William Merritt noted, "The only Black teacher we had in the high school had encouraged me to go to college, let me know I could go, and told me where to apply. Once he did that, he, his family, and the church made sure that I had support to do that."[4] This sentiment was prevalent among many leaders, who noted that particular teachers took interest in them and helped nurture their development. Reatha Clark King, who attended school in the previously mentioned one-room church that doubled as a school house in Pavo, Georgia, fondly remembered her teachers. She recalled one individual who travelled over 200 miles each week to ensure that local children received an education, as there were no other teachers in the area. This teacher not only taught them lessons but also built their self-esteem: "[She] just noted how studious we were and how able we were so we got that encouragement from day one to use our abilities. We would soak up everything she could teach us and be in a position to help the [other] school students, as well."[5] The Denver Foundation leader Lauren Y. Casteel also noted the significance of an

African American teacher when she first attended an elite private school in Cambridge, Massachusetts. Adjusting to the predominantly White environment might have been difficult but for the help this teacher offered. She reportedly told Casteel's parents, "Don't worry, leave her to me." She mentored and challenged the second grader, who now fondly recalled her impact, saying:

> She opened up a sense of intellectual curiosity for me that remains to this day. She gave me a sense of belief in my capabilities and sense of security in what could have been a really [difficult] situation going from segregated Atlanta to Cambridge [Massachusetts]. I mean just the weather alone. There was snow. My whole world changed to this predominantly White world, intellectual world, and it was sort of more international . . . I learned to love to learn. Betty Rawlins was my s/hero. I went to see her as an adult, and it was great just to thank her.[6]

In high school, Emmett D. Carson reported having "ample counseling support" and "the best teachers teaching AP courses after suddenly being transferred out of a regular homeroom and placed into a new one with 'geek kids.' "[7] This new access gave him and a few others college-focused academics and experiences that enabled them to excel and that were not available to the majority of public school students.

That said, things were not always perfect. A number of respondents faced discrimination in their school environment. As mentioned above, Heather Arnet felt "unsupported" in the Jewish day school she attended in Miami, Florida.[8] Citing a misogynistic religious culture in the school, she felt that her brother received more opportunities and support as a boy than she was given as a girl. Other respondents told of discrimination they experienced on the basis of race. As noted in Chapter 3, Joseph L. Smith encountered a very hostile group of teachers when he was among the first students to integrate a Catholic elementary school in Indianapolis in 1949.[9] And William Merritt found no support academically among the White teachers and administrators in his high school in 1950s Plainfield, New Jersey.[10] Interestingly, Merritt did find support for his participation in sports. Overall, however, negative situations in school were atypical and relationships with teachers were strong; as Dwayne Ashley noted, "I still have relationships with my teachers [today]."[11]

Guidance Counselors: Friend or Foe?

Although many educators were a blessing in the lives of the leaders, encouraging them to pursue their dreams, others were "dream stealers."[12] Several of the leaders reported difficulty with high school guidance counselors on the questions of whether and how to go to college. These individuals felt that guidance counselors grossly underestimated their academic abilities and tracked them toward less prestigious institutions. Alica Dixon had an unsupportive guidance counselor who told her that she would not be accepted into a certain college. "My response was just give me the [college's] phone number, I don't accept your opinion."[13] She was accepted to the University of California, San Diego, and graduated. Other respondents, including Yvette Desrosiers-Alphonse (an honor roll student), were placed into an educational track for junior college or vocational college when they, in fact, were interested in a four-year higher education. Desrosiers-Alphonse's mother had to intervene in order to get her placed into the college preparatory track.[14] She was counseled to attend state university, but eventually earned a master's degree from the University of Chicago. Conversely, Erica Hunt was recognized as a gifted student and given many opportunities for college preparation as a result; however, she also clearly observed how other classmates were discouraged and neglected, when she stated that "there is a real scarcity of career guidance or counseling. In fact, the usual habit pattern is to tell people what they can't do and what they can't be."[15]

Perhaps the clearest account of unsupportive counsel was given by William Merritt. He described receiving mixed messages from White administrators, until finally a Black teacher pointed him in the direction of higher education:

> A White vice principal said he had worked at Virginia State College and he told me that there were Black colleges that I could

probably get into. I went to the counselor after he told me that and he discouraged it . . . At the same time . . . they hired a Black phys ed teacher who was from Virginia and graduated from Virginia State. He changed life for us in that school. He told every Black person that you can and should go to college.[16]

Merritt clearly links his bad experience with a guidance counselor to race. The White staff at his school was ambivalent about Black students' career ambitions; it took a Black teacher, Merritt felt, to understand how important college attendance was for the Black students.

Some respondents reported having guidance counselors who were helpful. As mentioned, Emmett D. Carson reported having "ample counseling experiences" and Carol Goss recalled a counselor and some teachers who took interest and "wanted to be sure that I was successful."[17] One leader fondly discussed her exceptional guidance counselor. She recalled,

[He] was very influential in how many of us ended up going to the colleges and universities that we did. He kind of said no bars, your grades, your scores, you're going to apply and we'll see how it falls. So it was sort of don't hold back, no holds barred, if this is where you think you'd like to go let's go there. Unlike I know a number of other cases where it was don't even think about it.[18]

Evidently, school support for these future leaders was uneven. Some had very supportive teachers and administrators; others did not. Certain of the leaders were discouraged from pursuing higher education, and in some cases this was clearly linked to race. In spite of the so-called guidance they received, all of the leaders persevered.

The Influence of Higher Education

Several major themes emerged across the interviews with regard to higher education. For most of the leaders, college was a given; their parents made it clear from an early age that they were expected to pursue higher education—even if they were going to be first in their family to earn a college degree. Although the respondents attended all types of institutions of higher education, quite a large majority enrolled in small, liberal arts colleges, with many attending women's colleges or historically Black college or universities. Majors in the humanities and the creative arts were quite common. A strong majority of the leaders were heavily involved in co-curricular activities in college, and many had a job either on or off campus. On the negative side, most of the leaders experienced race or gender discrimination of some kind during college.

College was always on the horizon for the majority of these leaders. They were encouraged by their parents to pursue higher education, and it was valued in their homes. For instance, according to Nancy Burd, "college was a given in my family. You went to college whether you could afford it or not."[19] For the most part, the leaders were influenced by their parents with regard to their college choice, but made the final decision themselves. Cummins Foundation leader Mindy McWilliams Lewis, for example, was strongly encouraged to pursue higher education, but not told where or what major to choose:

> My parents were very insistent that we get an education and that we do our best, whatever that meant, and that we worked hard at fulfilling our greatest potential. They didn't have any expectations necessarily that we pursue one career versus another but they wanted us to pursue what we felt was important to us and that we did it grounded in education.[20]

In some instances, these leaders' parents pushed them to choose a more elite school or a school that was farther away from home and would offer them the opportunity to expand their horizons. Although many of the leaders came from middle-income homes, their parents were concerned about paying for college and urged them to pursue degrees at institutions that gave the most scholarship money.[21]

As mentioned, most of the leaders graduated from small, liberal arts colleges. Many of these were in the Northeast or the South.

With very few exceptions, these leaders pursued majors in the arts, humanities, or social sciences and were also involved in creative pursuits. Many of the leaders were interested in acting, singing, and the arts, although they opted to major in areas such as political science, English, and history. Overwhelmingly, they were focused on exploring ideas and not merely on making money, which fits squarely with their decision to pursue employment within the nonprofit sector.

It should be noted that a number of the respondents had significant educational experiences outside school. For example, before enrolling at Swarthmore College, Lauren Y. Casteel spent a summer in Eastern Europe—during the height of the Cold War. With Soviet tanks stationed in Czechoslovakia in the wake of the 1968 uprising, she experienced the brunt of communist oppression. The European trip gave her a different perspective on democracy and race relations in the United States:

> I developed an enormous appreciation for democracy, and as I watched people on bread lines and students would whisper to us on darkened corners for fear of people being overheard, I developed an even deeper appreciation for free speech. While on one hand I had been at home protesting the war, and civil rights, and social justice issues, and marching out of high school, and slapping "Free Angela" stickers on the refrigerator door, and wearing my dashikis and my dishans and my Afros ten feet wide and all of that, I thought, "Wow at least I can do that."[22]

Yvette Desrosiers-Alphonse, on the other hand, volunteered at community health centers while working on her master's degree at Boston University. After completing the degree, she joined the Peace Corps and worked in the Jamaican health system for two years. These experiences pushed her career focus toward bringing access to health care in disadvantaged regions.

Of note, six of the leaders attended historically Black colleges or universities and had wonderfully rich and meaningful experiences. They were empowered and nurtured to be leaders in the future. Their experiences played a significant part in their choice to pursue leadership roles in nonprofit institutions. In Emmett D. Carson's words,

> Morehouse has this tradition of we're the best. We're the best. And if you get through Morehouse, you're one of the best . . . Morehouse had the view when I was there that they would make us into diamonds. You're coal right now. You're just a lump of coal. And we've got to put so much pressure on you that we're . . . we're going to turn you into a diamond. And if you're a diamond, then we can send you out there into this cold, hard world and you will survive and you will shine.[23]

Susan Taylor Batten, of the Annie E. Casey Foundation, learned about issues facing African American communities at Fisk University, and the institution nurtured her interest in policy and how it shapes Black communities. Batten said that Fisk empowered her, in that "it was really important for me to be in a school that basically had high expectations and demonstrated that no matter what African Americans can succeed."[24]

Those African American leaders who attended Black colleges were fortunate in that they did not have to contend with White racism on a regular basis.[25] For example, according to Phillip Thomas at the Chicago Community Trust, who attended Morehouse after transferring from a historically White institution, "Once at Morehouse, I pretty much did whatever I wanted to with no barriers and after my experience in an all White institution, I think I started to develop a whole lot more confidence. And started to see myself in more realistic ways."[26] Dwayne Ashley had a similar experience at Wiley College and remarked that he owed a debt to his professors. Specifically, Ashley remembered, "They believed in you, they told you that you had to be the best, and they expected it. You knew that because you attended that institution and they talked about the fact that it was the oldest Black college in Texas and all of the people who came to that school, you had to achieve. You were carrying on a legacy and that was drilled in you every day."[27] The experiences of the leaders who attended historically Black colleges and universities are consistent with those of other Black college graduates. Overwhelmingly, graduates describe Black colleges as nurturing, supportive, empowering, and free of White racism.[28] These leaders' Black college experiences go hand in hand with the Cross and Tatum notion of immersion, discussed in Chapter 2: the college provided an opportunity for involvement with "everything related to their race" and for social-izing "within their particular racial group," in a place that was safe from stereotypes and allowed for positive self-development.[29]

Their counterparts at historically White institutions certainly did not experience a stereotype-free environment, and the aggres-sions they endured shaped their worldview. For example, the Sister Fund executive director Kanyere Eaton recalled this very unwelcoming experience when she arrived at Cornell University:

> It was extremely White. White men, I think, were extremely enti-tled. It was my first real honest to God encounter with racism and with White male privilege . . . I was shocked by their boldness and sense of entitlement. My freshman year I moved into a dorm with a White woman. I was assigned a room with a White woman from Dryden, New York, which was the Klan headquarters. She was a nice person. But a guy on the floor came and sat on my bed maybe two months in and said, "Kanyere, we like you." I said "I'm glad. I like you too." He said, "We didn't think that we would, of course." I said, "Why is that?" He said, "Because you're Black."[30]

Eaton goes on to explain that her encounter with racism at Cornell strongly influenced her identity and interests:

> I became aware of myself as a Black woman on the cam-pus . . . I became aware, I think, for the first time of the real relevance of race issues, the real relevance of gender issues. I got more of that in graduate school. I really identified much more powerfully as a Black woman as a result of being awash in White privilege and being aghast at the audacity of it, the audacity of it.[31]

Eaton's strong race and gender consciousness continued to sur-face in her career directions, first in her job as director of social services at the Riverside Church in New York City and later as the executive director of the Sister Fund.

Another factor in the college experience of the respondents—and one that influenced their career direction—was participation in co-curricular activities. Research shows that young people who are actively engaged in such activities are not only likely to do well in college but are also more likely to continue similar involvement as adults.[32] The leaders in this study were thoroughly engaged in their colleges, just as they were at the secondary school level. Most were involved in student government, Black student organizations, fraternities and sororities, or debate teams. Of note, many of the leaders were active in volunteer efforts. For example, Dwayne Ashley of the Thurgood Marshall College Fund was the president of the National Pre-Alumni Council. This organization is part of the United Negro College Fund (UNCF) and works with Black college students to increase giving among the student population and to inculcate philanthropic values.[33] In Ashley's words, "I oversaw the pre-alumni giving and activities for all of the UNCF colleges, so I started to get introduced to fundraising as an undergraduate. I set it as a goal because I was so impressed with the UNCF; I wanted to work with them."[34] The Missouri Foundation for Health program officer Jasmine Ratliff volunteered with Big Brother/Big Sisters while in college. According to Ratliff, "I had a little sister in Charlottesville. That exposed me to lower income living and literally, those I met lived on the opposite side of the tracks [from the university]—literally that side of the tracks."[35] Heather Arnet volunteered in areas that spoke to her feminist mentality. She worked at the women's center on her campus and did volunteer work for Planned Parenthood.[36]

Certain leaders' student involvements set a pattern for conscientious leadership in the nonprofit and philanthropy world. For example, Emmett D. Carson recalls being a thorn in the side of the establishment at Princeton University:

There were people in that system who said, "Who does he think he is? . . . He gets here, and he starts the Black Graduate Caucus. How is he a graduate student with time to do this? He gets money from outside the school to do a conference through the Black Graduate Caucus on affirmative action and brings in these national speakers . . . He's bringing all these national people to talk about affirmative action." So what I was trying to do was create a culture to talk about issues of race.[37]

Carson goes on to explain that the "talk about issues of race" involved criticism of Princeton's status quo:

When I was there, the class of, what was it, '55, had their alumni reunion. They did a survey of them. Sixty-four percent of the class of '55 thought that African Americans were less qualified than White students to be at Princeton. And so a group of us got these white buttons made up that said "We find 64 percent of the class of '55 offensive."[38]

Significantly, Carson's activist stance did not end at Princeton. He went on to hold key positions at the Ford Foundation and the Minneapolis Foundation, and ultimately to be the CEO of the Silicon Valley Community Foundation. He also was chair of the Council on Foundations and helped create the Louisiana Disaster Recovery Foundation, serving as its executive director, in the wake of Hurricane Katrina. Of his leadership approach in these various positions he said, "I have been outspoken during most of my career."[39]

The experiences of both Eaton and Carson provide a nice illustration of the kind of race- and gender-specific socialization discussed in Chapter 2. Each had an encounter with racism as a student. And each leader's career path resulted in what Cross and Tatum described as internalization and commitment—finding ways to "translate a personal sense of racial [gender] identity into ongoing action."[40] As these two leaders were among the younger generation of interviewees, Eaton's and Carson's experiences also provide insight into the type of discrimination present in today's educational system. Neither was denied a place in the university because of race; however, each confronted lingering assumptions of inferiority and felt an extra obligation to prove his or her worth within the academic world.

Overall, there were many similarities in the educational experiences of the leaders interviewed for this study. They were leaders early on, taking positions in student government and leading co-curricular activities both in high school and college. Their choice of higher education institution leaned toward the liberal arts college, with many majoring in the humanities or social sciences. Most often, their parents were strongly supportive of their educational ambitions. What differed was the amount of support they received from teachers and administrators at various levels. In some cases the educational environment they encountered was strongly supportive and nurturing; in others it was downright hostile. Either way, the educational setting was a place where race and gender consciousness took form and led, in many cases, to a long-term commitment to social engagement in the nonprofit or philanthropic world.

CHAPTER 5

Religion and Spirituality

Justice, justice you shall pursue.

—Deuteronomy 16:20

Let those who give alms, both men and women, and lend unto Allah a goodly loan, it will be doubled for them, and theirs will be a rich reward.

—Qur'an 57:18

All of the world's religions ask their followers to give of themselves through wealth and service. Whether according to the concept of *tzedakah* in Judaism, the idea of charity in Christianity, or the belief of *zakat* in Islam, there is an understanding that anyone, no matter how meek, can give of himself or herself to help others. Religion's influence on American philanthropy predates the founding of the country by over a century. The first solicitations of education, hospitals, and support for the underprivileged were all made by clergy or on behalf of the church.[1] How does religion influence the current generation of America's foundation and nonprofit leaders? And how, in particular, does it affect the lives and careers of Black and female leaders? This chapter explores the influence of religion on the work of those who engage in philanthropy professionally. We begin with a brief look at how the major religions engage in philanthropic giving.

Giving in the Major Religions

Within Judaism the idea of philanthropy is encapsulated in the Hebrew word *tzedakah*. Originating from the root *tzedek*, meaning righteousness, fairness, or justice, the concept of *tzedakah* is not viewed as a generous act; it is simply an act of social justice. There is a strong history of progressive philanthropy and support of social justice in the Jewish community. Traditional Jewish philanthropy rests on the concept of *tikun olam*, repairing the broken world, and *gemilut chasadim*, literally "bestowing kindnesses," and translated as benevolence—both being principles that extend to helping Jews and non-Jews alike.[2]

Christianity, like other faiths, has an understanding of charity in the context of "almsgiving." For example during Lent, the liturgical period leading up to Easter, Christians traditionally pray, alter their food consumption, and give alms (money or goods) to those in need. However, charity in Christianity is more than an obligation or duty. The word "charity" is first used in the New Testament as a word for love. "A Christian understanding of charity is far more radical and demanding than simply giving from what we have 'left over,'" as almsgiving would suggest.[3] Linda Jones stated, "Charity, for Christians, is not a demeaning hand-out; it is a vibrant expression of love."[4] The Judeo-Christian religions have the concept of tithing, or giving 10 percent of one's annual income to others in need.

Philanthropy within the Muslim tradition is one of the five pillars, or personal obligations, of the faith. *Zakat*, or almsgiving, is generally seen as a function of tithing where Muslims donate 2.5 percent of their annual wealth. *Zakat* is often viewed as compulsory, while *sadaqah*, a close Arabic word to the Hebrew *tzedakah*, is voluntary giving for social welfare.

The influence of religion on the leaders interviewed for this study is remarkable. Only two of the executives were not brought up in a faith community. Many of the foundation leaders remarked that involvement in a religion—and in particular the example set by family members who gave through their religious institution—created a basis for their philanthropic actions later in life.

Parental Influence through Religion

One form of parental modeling, as described earlier in Chapter 3, was giving to the church. Emmett D. Carson's work as well as others' finds that religion plays an important role in the philanthropic decisions of African Americans.[5] Building on this literature, Noah D. Drezner's research shows the continued importance of the African American church to philanthropy in the millennial generation (consisting of those born between 1982 and 2001).[6] As that institution was significant in the lives of many of the respondents to this study, this chapter will provide detailed information about the Black church and its giving traditions.

In another study, Hodgkinson and Weitzman show that those who had witnessed family members helping others were themselves more likely to make charitable contributions than those who had not (73.6 percent versus 50.0 percent). Other scholars emphasize adult influence in teaching the value of philanthropy.[7] Drezner's study found that student donors to private historically Black colleges and universities were influenced by parental and guardian philanthropic behavior.[8] The parental modeling described extended beyond the traditional nuclear family to include relatives, close family friends, and religious figures. This study finds that the extension of the larger family's effect is consistent with research on philanthropy within minority communities.[9]

Using the Center on Philanthropy Panel Study (COPPS), Wilhelm, Brown, Rooney, and Steinberg found that parents' giving to church, synagogue, or mosque is strongly correlated to their children's giving to religious institutions. COPPS is currently the only dataset that links the charitable giving of both parents and children. Further, their study found that parents' philanthropy toward religion is "positively associated with children's secular giving, but in a more limited sense" than that of children's giving to religious organizations.[10] In other words, "children whose parents give to religious purposes give more to secular purposes (about one-third more in terms of the marginal effect on observable secular giving), but the amount children gave to secular causes did not increase in proportion to the amount their parents gave to religious causes."[11] Nevertheless, it is clear that the power of parental giving to religion has a significant effect on the giving behaviors of children. The Independent Sector reported similar findings regarding religious giving and volunteering for religious and secular nonprofits.[12]

Parental and close-relative philanthropic modeling through religion was notable throughout the responses of the foundation and nonprofit leaders who participated in this study. Of particular interest was the number of participants in this study who indicated that they had clergy in their family. Whether ministers, bishops, or pastors, over half of those interviewed noted that they had at least one, sometimes more, clergy in their close or nuclear family. Still others noted that their parents were lay leaders within their church.

Yvette Desrosiers-Alphonse stated that since her father and grandfather were Methodist ministers, philanthropy, in terms of money and service, was expected in her family. She recalled that "we would get our allowance and you were expected to tithe. But we also did a lot of mission work."[13] She was taught early on to give to those less fortunate. Desrosiers-Alphonse recalled one Christmas when her parents told her, "This Christmas we're going to have a different Christmas. We are going to serve. You were put on this earth to serve and to help. Your fixation on the toys and all the things that we thought were important for Christmas needs to shift."[14] When she asked what would come of her presents, she recalls being told, "You can take two with you but we'd like you to think about giving the rest away to a child who won't have any presents this Christmas."[15] That experience affected Desrosiers-Alphonse profoundly; she noted, "Ever since [then] my family has not bought into the idea that at Christmas you need to buy things. Instead we do things for each other or give gifts of meaning...So I think that's how [giving] cultivated in us that you need to give back and you need to do."[16] Desrosiers-Alphonse's experience is an example of parental modeling and the effects of discussing the philanthropic act. As noted in Chapter 3, the combination of modeling and awareness created the greatest likelihood of philanthropic giving in children.

Desrosiers-Alphonse's experience follows a pattern for those raised in the African American church. According to Holloman, Gasman, and Anderson-Thompkins, the church had a unique role because of its history as the first Black-controlled organization in the United States. The first African American church was founded during the colonial period by free Blacks in Philadelphia. These individuals had been excluded from the White Methodist church and decided to pool their resources to form their own house of worship, which they called the African Methodist Episcopal (A.M.E.) Church. Thus, the need for giving was established early on, both as charity and as a political act: in order to bring justice to Blacks in America, one had to give. That this giving tradition continues in recent times is evident from a 1998 Lilly Endowment study of Black church congregants, in which 96 percent of respondents said that giving to the church regularly was important and 85 percent said that tithing, or giving one-tenth of one's income, was essential.[17]

Caprice Bragg, vice president for gift planning and donor relations at the Cleveland Foundation, had a different but equally compelling experience growing up in the Catholic Church. She recalled a "whole sort of lessons around philanthropy rooted in what you see in church."[18] Bragg attended Catholic schools that focused on service to others; she spoke of her first "work" experience being volunteering in local retirement homes. The emphasis on service and giving within the church made a strong impression on Bragg. Morris Price, of the Gill Foundation, was brought up within a family committed to church-based giving. He was required to tithe beginning in first grade. However, he did not make the connection between this type of contribution and philanthropy:

> Tithing was a given, but I never knew that was considered philanthropy or charity, but that's what you were supposed to do.

So when my mom and dad gave us our allowance, ten percent of that had to be set aside to go to church that Sunday. So it was built in automatically. I don't know if any of us thought this was philanthropy. I just thought that was what your mom and dad told you to do and so you did it.[19]

Without this connection—the connection between the gift itself and the notion of helping humanity—there was diminished likelihood of church-based philanthropy leading to further philanthropic involvement.[20] As will be discussed in the next section, for respondents such as Price, the connection between religion and philanthropy was not made through tithing so much as through a commitment to social justice.

The modeling of prosocial behaviors was not always as sophisticated or deep as in Desrosiers-Alphonse's recollections. Yet the acts still led to a lasting effect. Reatha Clark King spoke about how her family modeled the importance of helping others in a simple, yet compelling, way.

Cash money was very scarce but they [my parents] did donate to the church. They passed the plate and you put something in. . . . The word "philanthropy" was not in the vocabulary. It was "giving" or "sharing" what you had. Either it was neighbor-to-neighbor sharing, very common for the lady next door not to have enough flour to make bread or biscuits, or enough cornmeal to make cornbread.[21]

The act of putting a small amount into the collection plate or helping the next-door neighbor with a cup of cornmeal was part of community building. It had a lasting effect on King's conceptualization of philanthropy regardless of whether the term was used or not. The fact that her family helped through "sharing" and noted the importance of that action by talking about it likely intensified the action's effect, in agreement with the findings of Bar-Tal, Bentley, and Nissan.[22]

Religion had an effect on some of the participants even though they described themselves as not being part of a faith community or having nonreligious parents. This was particularly true for those participants who were Jewish. This might be a result of the fact that Judaism is viewed by many as both a religion and an ethnicity with a distinct culture that is not necessarily tied to religious practice.[23] Heather Arnet recounted that her parents had been brought up as Orthodox Jews but lapsed in their religious practice. One practice that they did preserve, however, was that of setting aside money for *tzedakah*, philanthropy, on Friday evenings as the Sabbath began—which according to Arnet "wasn't an option."[24] This weekly ritual, as well as other activities within her Jewish upbringing, taught Arnet the "concept of charitable work and a requirement, regardless of where you were on the economic strata, there was always someone lower that you were supposed to give to."[25]

Nancy Burd also learned the importance of philanthropy through cultural Judaism rather than religious practice. The Philadelphia Foundation vice president spoke of a relationship with Judaism that had little to do with God:

> We acknowledge our religion and we're very conscious of it and we would hope that our daughter will marry in the religion. However, we are not religious people. We don't talk about God. We don't think about God quite the same way that other people do who are religious. My husband's parents were Holocaust survivors so there is a sense, at least for him, that there is no God. His religion comes from the fact that they were Jewish and as a result of being Jewish they were in the Holocaust. Ninty-five percent of their family died. So they're coming out of it from a very different perspective than the way I grew up as a Jew.[26]

Although they do not have a traditional view of religion, Burd and her husband still value being part of the Jewish community, as evidenced by their wanting their daughter to marry within the faith. Burd acknowledged that Judaism's teachings on the importance of helping others had made an impression on her as a child.

Social Justice Modeling

Like philanthropic modeling, social justice beliefs and actions can be modeled and can affect others' prosocial behaviors. David Rosenhan found that deeply committed and involved civil rights volunteers had their sense of action and volunteerism as a result of their home environment.[27] Additionally, Gregory L. Cascione found that family influences and experiences affect the motivations of major gift donors within higher education.[28] He noted:

> Participation drew directly from their family backgrounds, [sic] and was assisted by the historical milieu in which they were living. Having individuals who are able to teach generosity through their actions and lifestyles plays a crucial role [in] carrying on a philanthropic tradition. Role modeling represents a form of teaching philanthropic values and individuals who represent such generosity encourage others by their actions. Extraordinary acts of generosity become ordinary events and since they are seen as ordinary events, the ability to replicate them would be a typical response in the course of an individual's life.[29]

Witnessing the involvement of others in social justice movements—such as the activism around civil rights—affects one's own philanthropic motivations. Many of the leaders interviewed for this project spoke of their religious experiences in the context of social justice and progressive rights movements. Some noted that their parents' involvement in the Civil Rights Movement in the 1960s was a key part of their upbringing, while others spoke about the importance of ongoing social justice and equality struggles. In many cases, religion had a role in these struggles. As at its earliest beginnings, the Black church during the civil rights era was a place where African Americans pooled their resources to resist oppression. Montgomery Alabama's Dexter Avenue Baptist Church, for example, was a rallying point for the 1955 bus boycott, which was the starting point for the Civil Rights movement. From the mid-1950s on, Martin Luther King Jr., himself a Baptist minister, visited churches throughout the South to rally congregations in support of the movement—and to plan protest actions.[30] That the church was critical to the movement was understood by not only congregants but racist opponents who targeted these institutions for attacks—as in the tragic 1963 Birmingham bombing of the 16th Street Baptist Church.

The Cummins Foundation's Mindy Lewis noted that church played a considerable role in her upbringing and understanding of philanthropy. Her church experience "had an impact in terms of our [her and her siblings] understanding of helping others, doing good, and to be thankful and blessed for whatever we were given."[31] In particular she spoke of how while she was growing up in the segregated South, the church's involvement in the struggles against Jim Crow had a lasting effect on her commitment to and understanding of the power of philanthropy. This effect on children of the Civil Rights Movement is consistent with that noted by Rosenhan and Cascione.[32] However, these two authors' works look at the decision to make philanthropic contributions. Lewis's experience motivated her to work in the nonprofit sector.

A number of participants stated that religious involvement early in life motivated them to take a stand as adults on issues of importance to them. These new causes—such as gay rights and feminism—were sometimes very different than the ones emphasized in their religious upbringing.

Morris Price of the Gill Foundation, the largest funder of gay and lesbian civil rights in the nation, combined the commitment to faith that he acquired from his parents and his dedication to rights for sexual minorities in his work. "Civil rights is civil rights. Access to me is access."[33] Price is the program officer working with communities of color, religion, and faith. He spends his time meeting with religious institutions, seminaries, and civil rights organizations and looks for intersections on how these organizations can work together. When describing the faith in his childhood, Price said that "the church was very consuming ... I felt very comfortable with faith."[34] Perhaps one reason the Gill leader described the African American church as such a sheltering institution was that it was home to an all-encompassing range of communal activities. According to Holloman et al., because African Americans were excluded from a host of White organizations, including labor unions and social organizations, they looked to the Black church to provide a social nexus. It was also a place of cultural ferment to which many well-known Black musicians trace their roots. Black ministers were known to be particularly effective in mobilizing their congregants to give, and for this reason philanthropy of all kinds took place there, including both monetary offerings and volunteering. Overall, the Black Church was the dominant institution in the socialization process for many African Americans.[35]

Because of the special place the church has in many African Americans' lives, outside philanthropy often looks to it as a conduit for giving within the Black community. Holloman et al. note that major foundations such as Lilly and Ford have undertaken antipoverty and educational efforts in collaboration with Black churches. The importance of the church in the community also explains why Price at the Gill foundation is working with Black churches on gay and lesbian issues, although Gill's goals may be in conflict with traditional church mores.

In their study of African American participation in the church, Ellison and Sherkat found that "throughout American history, the Black church has occupied a distinctive position in the individual and collective lives of African Americans."[36] This distinctive position was evident in the responses of numerous African Americans interviewed for this study.[37] But beyond simply giving to those in need, there was a sense of connection between the church, philanthropy, and social justice. This is in agreement with the recent work of Harold Dean Trulear, who argues, "In many communities, the leadership of both the religious community and the local NAACP was one and the same, challenging the notion of a deradicalized Black church, and replacing it with the more nuanced view that churches often supplied the spiritual and moral vision for persons to exercise social advocacy work through secular organizations."[38]

Kanyere Eaton, the executive director of the Sister Fund, has been deeply affected by her Christian faith and its teachings about helping others through philanthropy. She acknowledges her faith as a formative experience in her life that led to a call to the ministry and her pursuit of the masters of divinity and social work degrees concurrently. Viewing need through the lens of Christianity led Eaton to understand poverty as an injustice.

Eaton said that the seminary "really helped me to see more about socioeconomic realities and ways that plain old flat out unleveled the playing field. The people weren't less ambitious, less hopeful, less dedicated. They just had much less opportunity, a very smaller view of what was possible for them."[39]

As a result of her upbringing within the church and her experiences with formal religious education, she decided to dedicate her career to helping others. As mentioned earlier, her first job after seminary and graduate school was at the Riverside Church in New York City. Eaton described her experience at Riverside as being a critical turning point in her career that gave her the chance to see up close what an engaged church could look like—a church engaged in its immediate community and the international community.[40] She characterized her work at the Sister Fund as being "led by God's spirit as much as I could perceive this was how God's spirit was leading me."[41] Eaton's experiences with both the Riverside Church and the Sister Fund point to a pattern described in Christopher Ellison and Darren Sherkat's research: African Americans are more closely affiliated with the church than are other Americans.[42] Research shows that African Americans often look to the church for advocacy, guidance, and the promotion of social needs within the community.[43] In turn, African American communities are highly committed to financially supporting the church.

Lauren Y. Casteel was drawn into social justice through her involvement in the Unitarian Church. "Much of the social justice movement originated within the context of the Unitarian Church and a very core teaching of tolerance and understanding of all faiths. [It] was incumbent upon us as individuals and communities to act upon that faith by promoting justice, and promoting tolerance, and promoting goodness and kindness."[44] Casteel was encouraged by her family and the church to help others in need. The modeling and education that she received regarding social justice led to her involvement in the nonprofit sector. She said that while she no longer attends church regularly she lives a life where she "no longer goes to visit God on Sunday. [She] walks with God all the time."[45] Consistent with the values she learned in her church, Casteel chose to serve as executive director of the Hunt Alternatives Fund, which is committed to the uplift of disenfranchised groups.

In the accounts of leaders such as Price, Eaton, and Casteel, we not only observed a connection between religion and the decision to engage in prosocial behavior but also the decision to pursue a career focused on social justice. These leaders learned to give at a young age as a result of their experience in the church. As they matured, they also learned to associate giving with social uplift and political liberation.

CHAPTER 6

Challenges and Sacrifices

For the leaders featured in this book, the road to success had many twists and turns. They came from different backgrounds—poor, rich; urban, rural—but all worked hard to attain higher education. All had supportive parents who taught them the value of working hard and actively encouraged them to succeed. Some landed in the philanthropy and nonprofit worlds after false starts in other arenas. Some turned their backs on more lucrative professions to make a career helping others. Most put in long hours at work, sometimes sacrificing contact with family and friends. One of the most common—and most interesting—themes was the complex role that race and gender played in these leaders' rise to the top. Many braved race and gender discrimination to arrive at their chosen profession, and in some cases it was discrimination that pushed them toward a career aimed at building a better world. A few acknowledged the difficulty of attempting to right the world's wrongs from within the privileged arena of philanthropy or the gnarled complexity of the nonprofit world.

For most respondents, a career in philanthropy or the nonprofit world was extremely demanding of time and energy. It meant less time spent for family, friendships, and personal enrichment. The 40-hour work week was unheard of in this group; most reported working 50, 60, or even 70 hours per week.[1] Many also reported spending long periods on the road—traveling to conferences or meeting with overseas contacts. For several respondents, the unspoken demands of the job required as much time as the explicit responsibilities. For example, Phillip Thomas had this to say about the sacrifices he made to move into his position as senior program officer for community development at the Chicago Community Trust:

> Breaking into foundations in a town like Chicago is kind of challenging, in any given year there just aren't many job openings, and I think one of the things that probably benefited me was the volunteer work, so that at any given time I've been on six boards, six different nonprofit boards, other volunteer activities and a lot of community meetings . . . That meant time away from my family. I've got small children, so you know, you sacrifice that.[2]

Caprice Bragg gave the following illustration of that very sacrifice:

> At the time my oldest was under a year old. I had been working the kind of hours where I really had not observed his development . . . But I came home and I saw him pull himself up in the crib. I kind of excitedly told my husband and he told me that my son had been doing that for a week.[3]

Looking back at her career, Denise McGregor Armbrister put it this way: "Would I have done it all over again? Probably, my children and family lost time with me and I lost time for me, I would want to recapture some of that time if I did it all over again"[4] Other respondents reported that their careers made a significant dent in their friendships and leisure activity. According to Heather Arnet, "I can't even tell you when it was the last time I went out with a friend for just a completely non-work-related drink—girls night out. I am a big yoga practitioner, and I fight to take a half-hour to go to a class once a month."

Previous research corroborates the stories these leaders tell. The "Ready to Lead?" study, for example, described how a younger generation in the nonprofit world is reluctant to take on the executive role. Among the 6,000 respondents to the survey, many cited an inability of directors to maintain a healthy work-life balance as a reason for not advancing to leadership positions. According to this study, "the long hours and compromised personal lives associated with executive leadership are significant deterrents to pursuing top positions."[5] Among those in the study who said they would definitely *not* pursue the executive director's role, the sacrifice of work-life balance was the second of the top five reasons cited.[6] One respondent to that study who felt discouraged about pursuing the director's role had this to say:

> My executive director's insane . . . is that where I'm going to be in 30 or 40 years? Is that where I'm headed, to be burnt out and working long hours and not seeing my kids grow up? But at the same time, where else do you pursue what you want to pursue?[7]

Pursuing what you want to accomplish—helping others, building a better world—is certainly the attraction of nonprofit work. But according to "Ready to Lead?" a widespread expectation still exists that such pursuits be undertaken with meager compensation:

> The wisdom on the streets—confirmed to some degree by this study—is that we tend to undervalue nonprofit work and the people who do it. Even those of us who should know better sometimes fall prey to the notion that important charitable work can and should happen at a discount. This same idea animates the view that professionals who toil at nonprofits ought to work longer hours and for less pay than their for-profit counterparts.[8]

Unlike this book, the "Ready to Lead" study was limited to nonprofit leaders and did not include foundation executives. Although they too work long hours, they are better paid than their nonprofit counterparts. Hence there were fewer complaints about salary and benefits. However, quite a number of respondents did muse about having turned down more lucrative careers to pursue the work they did. Among the respondents who had earned degrees in highly competitive fields were Dwayne Ashley, who received a master's in governmental administration from the University of Pennsylvania; Reatha Clark King, a Ph.D. in chemistry from the University of Chicago; and Emmett Carson, a Ph.D. in public and international affairs from Princeton University.

William Merritt, executive director of the Black United Fund, has a social work degree from Rutgers; about the other paths he could have taken, he says that "sometimes I talk to people at corporate [jobs]. They can't understand why I didn't go into corporate America where I could have made much more money and received many offers."[9]

Certainly, the nonprofit and foundation world demands quite a bit of its executives, and the group that participated in this study was no exception. As women and members of minority groups, however, they experienced problems with overwork more acutely than White men. Many entered the profession with an extra dose of drive born of the notion that they would have to try harder to get ahead. As noted in Chapter 3, some experienced discrimination directly during childhood. Others felt it indirectly, as fallout from a society that acknowledged the importance of equality but not the depth of inequality to which minorities had been subjected. They all, to a greater or lesser degree, understood that that its effects would be felt as they moved through their careers. The anxieties they felt over having to struggle just to keep up come to light in the interviews.

Contact with Whites made the respondents aware of their status in society and of the problems of racism in the United States and helped cement their ethnic identity. For Reatha Clark King, the Jim Crow South enforced a strict racial etiquette even as it insinuated racial inferiority. Here again is a discussion of character traits that were expected of her as a young person—a discussion that hinges on the word "lazy":

> Mostly these were norms of community behavior: being friendly, outgoing to people, not meeting a stranger, speaking to people, acknowledging people when you see them, not being aloof, not being stuck up—that was the language. Also being smart and being willing to work and to work hard, not being lazy. That was a terrible word—lazy[10]

King shows that she was not only conditioned to be demur when interacting with Whites, but also trained by those close to her to react against myths of lower intelligence and laziness among African Americans. As mentioned in Chapter 3, overachievement was the only bulwark against such myths. As a result of racism, William Merritt also experienced lowered expectations in public schools he attended in Plainfield, New Jersey. According to Merritt, "it got to the point where you really didn't try hard... I wanted to be a scientist, but I didn't think that was something that was available to me." In fact, as mentioned in Chapter 4, a guidance counselor discouraged him from attending even a historically Black college or university.[11]

While diminished expectations, and even a diminished stature within society, were part of the formative years for these African Americans raised in segregated America, so was a separate sense of pride and a knowledge that some had succeeded in spite of all odds being against them. This pride was instilled by parents and other African American adults in the community who taught them to believe in themselves and work hard. The importance of such mentors in the psychosocial development of women and minorities is described in Chapter 2, which notes that a supportive role model can ameliorate the effect of the racial encounter. For William Merritt, for example, the Black physical education teacher mentioned in Chapter 3 was such a person. Before this teacher arrived, few Black students in the Plainfield, New Jersey, school were encouraged to pursue a college education. With his presence, momentum built and "the group before me about four went to college. Then the next year, in our senior year, something like ten [students] went. It went on and on."[12] Examples like this one not only allowed minority students to get ahead, they also created an intense desire in some of the respondents to follow in their footsteps—to be the one person in the neighborhood or the office who cast away barriers and let the next generation succeed. This idea is borne out by the evidence from the aforementioned study "Ready to Lead?" Minority respondents in this study were 10 percent more likely to be motivated by a desire to improve social conditions and help their community.[13]

The mentor or parent in the minority community who built the sense of pride and expectation in the child would also, in many cases, convey the idea that to get ahead, African Americans had to work harder than Whites. This was true regardless of whether the respondent came from middle-class or impoverished circumstances. As noted earlier in the book, Emmett Carson was told that he "needed to be twice as good to get half as much,"[14] and Karen Kelley Ariwoola was told that "you have to be better than everyone else."[15] In fact, it was a dual notion of race pride and race consciousness that many of these young leaders carried with them as they advanced through their careers: that on the one hand, it was possible to succeed if one tried hard, yet on the other, the system was patently unfair to African Americans and would place in front of them hurdles that others would not have to face. The "Ready to Lead?" study also alludes to this problem by noting that women and people of color tended to believe that they needed more education to succeed than Whites. Pointing to a higher number of minorities than White men who felt they needed more preparation before taking on a leadership role, the authors surmise,

> We might attribute these disparities as a response to the fact that white men are disproportionately represented in top-level management positions, making women and people of color feel the need to overprepare in order to counter their perceived disadvantages.[16]

Emmett D. Carson was clearly able to succeed in spite of any extra hurdles he faced. Regarding his accomplishments, he says,

> Things that people don't do until they are much later in their careers, I've already done. Very few people can say they've been president of two major foundations. I've written over a hundred articles. I've given I don't know how many speeches—international speeches—that are still quoted by people in those countries who are saying it has reshaped how they do their philanthropy.[17]

He goes on to mention honorary degrees from Indiana University, Morehouse College, and National Hispanic University. Perhaps his proudest moment was being "loaned" out by the Minneapolis

Foundation to the Louisiana Disaster Recovery Foundation, where he was interim executive in the wake of Hurricane Katrina. Yet all of these accomplishments came at a cost. For Carson, the forbidding landscape of racism came into focus when he enrolled in the Ph.D. program at Princeton's Woodrow Wilson School of Public and International Affairs. According to the scholar and foundation leader, "Let me say this: Princeton was a place where race became an issue." He arrived at the Ivy League institution as one of a few Black students from the South, and a graduate of the historically Black Morehouse College, where he received a great deal of support and encouragement from his professors. Carson continues, "And now suddenly I'm thrust into this White world where they look at you and say 'why are you here? And what makes you think that you at all can be successful with us?'" Describing his experience at Princeton, Carson frequently used words such as "war" and "trauma." As an example of the kind of treatment he faced, Carson mentioned a qualifying Ph.D. oral econometrics exam in which three professors grilled him, asking him to produce equations and explanations. According to the foundation leader, no other student was required to complete such an exercise.[18]

Carson was fully cognizant of the benefits of his Princeton education. He admitted that his career would not have advanced in the same way—that he would not have enjoyed the same connections and "cache" had he attended a less prestigious school. Moreover, he acknowledges that Princeton's wealth worked to his advantage. Because of his generous aid package, he was not saddled with student loans upon graduation and therefore could afford to take on jobs with less pay but greater personal reward. However, he believed that he could have attained the same benefit with less trauma. According to Carson, "it was brutal. And it was unnecessarily brutal, and in part it was brutal because of my race." Others noticed the effect it had on him:

My father used to say "you had a sense of humor until you went to Princeton." Because it was war. And you don't come back from war joking and laughing, and it's like every moment there are snipers out there. And the snipers can shoot at anything that moves, and I've got people writing memos who I don't even know, because I haven't even had a class from them.[19]

As Carson was able to fend off the attacks from these unseen sources, he did not allow them to handicap his career. Ultimately, the toll was on his psyche and interpersonal relationships. This is the only area in which he expresses regrets about his past:

> Personal relationships and balance are important. And it's funny, I'm now in the Silicon Valley and I meet many entrepreneurs who've been enormously financially successful at a young age. What I often hear from them is the same thing I feel myself which is they didn't have a lot of balance, and they talk about how they tell the younger guys who are working 24/7 to come up with the newest doohickey that everybody can't live without. However, if they were to go home and have dinner with their wives or you see their kids more at the soccer game or whatever, they would still come up with the device. It might take them a year longer . . . but they would be much healthier people.

Of course, Carson was not a computer "geek" driven by the need to innovate nonstop. What led him to want to work "24/7" was likely the challenge born of his parents' expectations: "Do as well as you can in school, be as successful as you can, always give 110 percent to every effort." Clearly, the need to give 110 percent was seen by his parents (both born in the Deep South) as a fact of life for an African American, an acknowledgement that society would overlook some of their best efforts. Looking toward his future, Carson now says, "I don't let the smaller things bother me. I don't necessarily give 110 percent to every effort." In a sense, Carson's experiences moving through the philanthropic world had a rather unphilanthropic effect. To help humanity, he had to work inhuman hours and harden himself against the others' attacks. Working overtime and fighting against racial barriers, he became a philanthropic warrior.

And this points to the most troubling kind of sacrifice in the philanthropic and nonprofit sector: the sacrifice of ends for means. As noted in the "Ready to Lead" study, "The genius of this sector—what continues to attract so many to nonprofit careers despite the potential disadvantages—is its promise of meaningful work leading to social change."[20] What happens when that meaningful work is diluted by the necessities of organizational function—the constant need, in a nonprofit, to raise funds, or in a grant-making institution, to promote an ideology of giving? Kanyere Eaton provides a nice illustration in recounting the direction her career took. As noted in Chapter 4, her move to New York to work as director of social services for Riverside Church was a watershed moment, a point at which her educational background as a divinity student, her personal background as a Black woman, and her daily work coalesced into a life calling:

> I realized that I cared profoundly about Black people . . . all of the poor people were Black. Everybody who was disenfranchised in the communities that I was serving, both in the soup pantry, clothing, direct service, welfare, in the public sphere and in the private sphere . . . Everybody looked like me.[21]

Speaking of her job at Riverside Church, she said, "It gave arms and legs to a fantasy of mine, put flesh and bones on it . . . I was there at a real needy time when we were having important conversations about how to launch our antipoverty work to another level."[22]

Later, she became executive director of the Sister Fund, enlisting faith communities in the uplift of women. Such a position would seem to be a locus of Eaton's personal interests—a commitment to social advancement and social justice underscored by an abiding faith in God. Yet hearing Eaton's description of her current work, it is hard not to call it mundane:

> We have two grant cycles. We produce two to three newsletters. We do some sort of special report every year. . . . We're always fielding questions about grants. In the last three years we've had a number of requests to speak publicly about what the foundation is doing. We're trying to promote an ideology.[23]

How successful has she been in promoting that ideology? Candidly, she states that it has been a difficult job: "The women's funding network hasn't always gotten what we're trying to focus on. Some faith based folks have been like 'I don't know. You're connected to the feminist movement, the feminists. The ungodly can't be trusted.'" But promoting the image of the group is what she does: "There's a way in which you just get consumed under whatever reputation the foundation has . . . It's not me. One thing I do is help to run a foundation. It's not me. It's a job." Summarizing what she has given up, Eaton states, "That's the biggest sacrifice, that I have not been able to give myself in these critical years to what I feel God created me to do though I feel this is probably and an important stepping stone."[24]

Similarly, many focus group participants in the "Ready to Lead" study expressed reluctance to take on a leadership role because it would take them away from what they loved most about nonprofit work: helping their community. According to one participant, "I enjoy working with the clients and working with people and doing a whole gamut of things other than just strictly working on fundraising and working with board members."[25]

Thus Eaton's frustration is like that of anyone who, from a position of direct engagement with a cause, moves up to one of leadership. Administering grant cycles, writing reports, fielding questions, promoting an ideology—this is the stuff of nonprofit and foundation leadership. To this list, we must add finance and fundraising responsibilities, which, according to the "Ready to Lead" study, was the top reason that rising nonprofit staff members opt not to pursue an executive director position.[26] A 2006 study titled "Daring to Lead," also by the Meyer Foundation and CompassPoint Nonprofit Services, notes, "Executives cited fundraising and finance as their least favorite aspects of their job and the areas in which they most needed to build their skills."[27]

A greater problem for women or minority leaders is becoming a functionary for the very system that one is trying to change. As one of Eaton's peers, the Annie E. Casey Foundation leader Susan Taylor Batten, points out, fixing a broken world is a difficult task to accomplish from a position of power:

I don't know if it's because of where I am right now but being in philanthropy, which is a very privileged industry, attempting to raise issues of equity and race is really tough. There are days when I think that it's somewhat of a contradiction to use the wealth of certain families in this country to try to address the inequity and wealth of others, but it's a pretty big challenge to do this work from the vantage point of philanthropy. At the same time, there's really no place else to do it unless you're in grassroots organizing.[28]

Such problems were quite pronounced for the foundation leaders interviewed for this study. Willis Bright, director of youth programs at the Lilly Endowment, stated that his biggest challenge was not to be a "purist," that is, not to be intolerant of the discrepancy between social justice goals and the fact that funding often comes from corporations with a checkered past regarding social justice.[29]

An added challenge for these minority and women leaders is how to cultivate the next generation—how to open the doors of the highest levels of leadership to those who have previously been excluded. Certainly, there has been progress in this direction: the United States now has a Black president, and as evidenced by the group of leaders participating in this study, quite a few minority and women leaders are watching over the coffers of wealth. One factor working in favor of minority leadership is the strong commitment by those who experienced race or gender discrimination in their own lifetimes. As mentioned above, the "Ready to Lead?" study found that people of color were 10 percent more likely to answer "definitely yes" or "probably yes" when asked if they would pursue the top leadership position in their organization; those who grew up poor were also more likely to say "yes" than those in the middle or upper classes.[30] For respondents in that study—as well as in the current one—the desire to groom future minority leaders was part of their motivation: "I would love to be that person that people look up to and for African American girls to say, 'Hey look, she's running a whole organization. This is something I can do as well.'"[31]

However, a close look at current statistics shows that minority coverage is spotty. White men still account for the largest share of foundation and nonprofit leaders, especially in the better-endowed organizations. Women are better represented, but not in the top-tier foundations and nonprofits.[32] Since the minority leader is often the first one of his or her kind to take on the executive role, he or she is considered somewhat of a novelty—a "statement," as Carson put it. When asked how race affected his experience in the workplace, he responded,

> I think it has both helped and hurt . . . people have looked at me and said, "well we want to make a statement by having an African American male that we think is capable and confident," and that has certainly helped me. I have been outspoken during most of my career, and so people have known what they were getting by hiring me, and so it was an intentional choice to do that. It has hurt, because there are people, when you decide to make a statement . . . who make your role much harder than it needs to be.[33]

For a member of a minority group, then, the executive's role is somewhat of a double-edged sword. His or her arrival heralds great expectations of change—both the ones he or she brings and those that the organization harbors. On the other hand, real efforts to enact change meet resistance. For the organization, the fact of having a minority or woman executive may be change enough. Returning to a topic discussed earlier in this book, this generation of minority and women nonprofit leaders were like the group of Black television and film pioneers that they revered as young people. Eager to take on significant parts, they were still largely confined to playing them in a way that was acceptable to a White audience, and within an industry that still existed for the benefit of Whites.

In fact, minority and women executives enter their roles with an enlarged vision—eyes open to the injustices in society that may be invisible to members of the dominant group. Often they come to the position with an extra-thick résumé, fortified against attacks on their competence that they have been trained to expect at any moment. Members of minorities especially have been taught by parents and mentors to give "110 percent" to any effort, and they know that lingering racism in our society will diminish what they have achieved. And they serve with a heightened sense of the influence they can have, in the organization itself, on the field in which they work and on future generations of minority and women nonprofit or foundation staffers.

The role they enter is rife with pitfalls. Previous studies of nonprofit leadership cited here describe a crocodile moat of problems for executives of all backgrounds: inhuman work weeks, diminished time with family and friends, lowered expectations regarding pay, and thorny relationships with boards of directors. Respondents in this study reported similar problems. What they also pointed to was an inherent structural impediment to the nonprofit or foundation as a change agent in society. To repeat the words of Susan Taylor Batten, "attempting to raise issues of equity and race is really tough" within the privileged world of philanthropy.[34] As we also learned from Kanyere Eaton, moving into a leadership role means that work becomes more abstract. Rather than helping people in need one helps the organization that is helping people in need. But what happens when helping the organization becomes its own justification?

Nonprofits and foundations, like other types of organizations, easily slip into a condition in which sustaining the system is the goal—where the means become the end. In the nonprofit world, one works tirelessly to raise funds—and soon enough, progress is measured by how much money is raised year in and year out, rather than how those funds are used to help people. In the foundation world, leaders carefully make the case—through well-polished reports, studies, and evaluations—that the wealth they control is being used to better humanity. How easily their leadership becomes a public relations exercise on behalf of that wealth, rather than an effort to help human beings. The challenge of "keeping it real"—making philanthropic work about the love of humankind—is all the more poignant for members of oppressed groups, who travelled an extra distance to arrive at their positions and brought with them a profound sense of the wrongs that afflict society. The next chapter will offer thoughts on how a new generation of women and minority leaders might answer the challenge of staying true to their ideals.

CHAPTER 7

Conclusion

Although these philanthropic leaders differ in terms of race, gender, geography, generation, and socioeconomic status, the similarities between them greatly outweigh the differences. Given their backgrounds, their ascent into leading roles within the foundation and nonprofit world makes sense. From their family and neighborhood environments to their schooling and community engagement, philanthropy has been a guiding theme throughout their lives. As one leader put it, "[Philanthropy] wasn't something separate from our lives. It was not like we do our life and then we go and be philanthropic. It was who we are. We are philanthropic people; that's what we do all the time. We were always thinking about how to help someone else."[1]

Patterns emerge in the life histories of these leaders that help us to understand how they became "philanthropic people." The process of socialization—the set of experiences that helped them to choose a direction in life—began in households and communities that were deeply affected by race and gender conflict, but that nevertheless gave positive messages to children about the possibility of success. Growing up, the respondents all had run-ins with racism or sexism. For African Americans of the earlier generation, such as Reatha Clark King and Joseph L. Smith, Jim Crow signs and the thinly veiled threat of violence gave a stern message about lines not to be crossed. For others, such as William Merritt or Heather Arnet, the encounter was in the form of discouraging words from teachers or guidance counselors about life options. These younger leaders also experienced racism, often as a veiled discourse that turned the notion of equality on its head. The glib substitution of sameness for equality—"colorblindness," as it were—became a popular way to turn a blind eye to women's and minorities' historical oppression. Such ideas were embedded in entertainment from the post-Civil Rights era (e.g., *I-Spy* and *Julia*), which tended to depict minorities as "just like you and me" save skin color. They acquired a political voice during the Reagan years, when it became popular to level charges of reverse discrimination at programs aimed at eliminating discrimination.

Later, these leaders found safe havens, places to socialize with members of their own race or gender and to share a common culture and common cause. For Dwayne Ashley and others, a historically Black college, an educational institution set up entirely to nurture Black scholarship, provided such a haven. For Yvette Desrosiers-Alphonse it was the AHANA house at the predominantly White Boston College. These leaders' experiences during their education—corresponding to the third or "immersion" stage of Cross and Tatum's five-stage schema—were critical to their decision to pursue a philanthropic career. By immersing themselves in their background, and meeting others who shared the same experience, they were able to develop the self-confidence necessary to face a world dominated by a culture different from their own. The respondents' testimony on this subject makes a strong case for classes, co-curricular activities, and even whole institutions focused on a particular race, gender, or ethnicity. Although debate rages about the value of such an approach—with some claiming that it hurts women and minority graduates' chances of success within the larger society—the leaders interviewed here were clearly *better* able to cope with the majority culture because of their immersion in the minority. As they moved toward adulthood, these individuals learned to channel their identification with a particular race or gender toward action in the larger world. This final phase of socialization resulted in the leaders' selection of careers in the nonprofit and foundation arena. In some cases, like that of

Kanyere Eaton, executive director of the Sister Fund, it meant working at an institution founded specifically to help causes with which the leader identified. In others, such as that of Emmett D. Carson, CEO of the Silicon Valley Community Foundation, it meant being an outspoken advocate for his group within an organization geared toward helping the general populace. In all of these cases, the path from childhood experience to adult socialization nicely followed the five-stage identity-formation patterns that William Cross and Beverly Tatum named in their writings.

Throughout the research, we found that these leaders were greatly shaped by historical events, including the Civil Rights Movement and the Women's Movement. These watershed moments served as an impetus for their pursuit of leadership roles in nonprofit organizations. The leaders grew up in periods of upheaval against societal norms, and as a result, many believed that they could break new ground. They looked to those near and far—everyone from television icons to teachers and parents—for role models, and more often than not, they were mentored through formidable periods. These role models were frequently—but not exclusively—the same gender or same race as their protégés. Nearly all of the leaders lived in homes in which their parents had high expectations, and they rose to meet the challenge of these expectations. Of note, many of the African American leaders felt the special obligation of representing not only their family but their race as a whole. This obligation could be a double-edged sword, as it put pressure on the respondents to perform *better* than their peers in an effort to prove the worth of their race or gender. Individuals like Emmet Carson reported the need for an extra-long résumé in order to deflect veiled assumptions of inferiority.

Respondents learned about philanthropy in formal and informal ways. Many, such as Morris Price or Reatha Clark King, witnessed family members performing simple acts of kindness in their communities—driving a stranger to church, offering food staples to neighbors without. Others participated in organized service activities, such as the circle of women described by

Carol Goss, who provided "cancer pads" to patients in need. And some participated in more conventional forms of philanthropy, through the collection plate at a church, for example. In many cases, church-based philanthropy had a social justice goal, as with those respondents whose churches supported civil rights protest.

These leaders were themselves highly engaged throughout their high school and college years—taking positions in student government, activist organizations, and serving their communities. Where there was no co-curricular activity that fit their interests, they would make one. Examples include the "Relief from Boredom" club, which one individual founded in high school as an arts-oriented alternative to sports, or the Black Graduate Caucus, which Emmett Carson helped found at Princeton University to promote dialog about racial issues. They tended to major in creative disciplines in college, rather than taking a straight and narrow path toward organizational leadership. For some, education came as much through travel or volunteer experiences as college itself. For Lauren Y. Casteel, for example, a trip to communist-ruled Eastern Europe reminded her that in spite of the history of troubled race relations at home, it was still possible to make a difference in the United States through free speech and the democratic process. Again, a high-quality education nurtured respondents' interest in philanthropic pursuits. Overall, these individuals had room in high school, college, and graduate school to develop visionary rather than just practical approaches to leadership.

For many—but not all—of the leaders interviewed, spirituality was also a spur to participation in philanthropic and nonprofit communities. Many parents and community members modeled philanthropy by giving through their church or other religious institution. Some went beyond simply asking children to contribute. In having their children give up Christmas presents for those in need, for example, Yvette Desrosiers-Alphonse's parents taught an object-lesson about the value of philanthropy. Whether it took place in the church, synagogue, mosque, or some secular context, philanthropy needed to be modeled.

For Black respondents in particular, the church was more than a place of almsgiving. It was seen as a nexus for social justice—a place that had nurtured the Civil Rights Movement. Mindy Lewis, for example, recalled the role of her church in civil rights struggles in the South, noting that it was an example of how philanthropy could make change. Respondents often cited the church as a reason for choosing social justice as a career. Thus religious institutions can inspire young people to pursue philanthropic careers when they model giving as a way to change society.

The leaders in this study clearly grew up with a different and more intense sense of who they were. In the academic arena, parents taught them to surpass competence and pursue excellence. They had a heightened awareness of injustice, including racial tensions and gender discrimination. Their notion of philanthropy went beyond charity to encompass changing the world. The mentors who helped direct them in their career choices left them with a sense that they, too, needed to be mentors to a new generation. Coming into leadership roles, the challenge they faced was to direct their intensity toward fixing the world—knowing the limitations of organized philanthropy and the demands it placed on its leadership. These limitations were particularly well known to the leaders, who came up through the highest echelons of power in the United States. For example, Emmett Carson's experience at Princeton University showed the effect of a more pervasive and insidious kind of racism than that embodied by a Jim Crow sign—the kind that worked behind closed doors, through subtle bias still prevalent among the White elites.

Overall, the individuals whose life and work is the focus of this study were very successful in meeting the enormous challenges they faced. Taking on roles that in many cases were hitherto unattainable for members of their race or gender, they made great progress in building a better world. What is clear from this research is that the leaders' ideas and values were instilled during their early years. Parents, teachers, and role models in their community taught them to be philanthropic and gave them a proper base from which to pursue leadership and activism. What is also clear is that they were driven in their careers to combat the still-pervasive effects of racism and sexism. This was chief among their reasons for joining the sector. The acknowledgment by all parties involved that such discrimination still exists is a prerequisite to maintaining a diverse nonprofit and philanthropic sector.

Epilogue

s someone who possesses an avid passion for literature, I confess a concomitant admiration for the epilogue. I relish the opportunity to absorb the words of authors—erudite or gritty—who hold court directly with the reader after the conclusion of some spellbinding tale. Of course, in the case of the preceding work, the fantastical and the fictional have been supplanted by the empirical and the editorial. Still, philanthropy remains, at its core, a love story as sweet as anything that romantic writers have ever dreamed up. This is not solely because of the etymological underpinning of the word (i.e., love and humankind). It is also because of the soft yet stubborn recognition that love confined to its noun form falls infinitely short of its potential; to be fully realized, love must always mature by becoming a verb. In short, love-as-verb is the *sine qua non* of true philanthropy. As many have pointed out, one can give without loving, but one cannot love without giving.

If people of color engage in philanthropy, will anyone notice? This question is intended to be much more than a riff on the well-worn philosophical brain teaser about an audience-less tree meeting its demise in some hypothetical woods. The fact is that philanthropy among people of color—"askers" as well as "givers"—very rarely is lauded in a manner that befits its history, its volume, and its impact. To be sure, proper recognition is neither a prerequisite nor a motivator for philanthropic activity among Americans of color (at least not to any greater degree than it is for White Americans). Still, I am hopeful that this small addition to the body of work regarding such philanthropy will spur yet more research, writing, teaching, and learning about this important topic.

In a real sense, this book is about heroes. Heroes are few and far between. To be clear, heroes are not simply mythical or mystical figments of our individual or collective imagination. They can be—and are—*ordinary* people who exhibit extraordinary commitment in service to others. People such as Oseola McCarty, Matel Dawson, and Albert Lexie are but a few examples of such heroes. Even though these men and women were born human, they become supernatural. I don't mean this in a metaphysical sense; I mean it in the sense that their actions will live well beyond their naturally appointed time in the earthly realm.

I realize that such language invites the risk of crossing the equally undesirable lines of hyperbole or cliché. Thus, I do not use the term "hero" lightly. I believe sincerely that there are a few individuals whose life and work merit such distinction. Their individual and collective actions bring to mind the Latin phrase *res ipsa loquitur*, which refers to something that speaks for itself.

The persons to whom I refer (even though we will ever know but a few of their names) remind us that we should not be merely dreamers of good *dreams*; we must also be doers of good *deeds*. As someone has said, we should not simply be humans *being*; we should be humans *doing*. They answer the call of what the Jewish faith refers to as *tikkun olum*—repairing the world. Or, in the words of Teddy Pendergrass, "the world won't get no better if we just let it be."

The great philosopher René Descartes offered a famous and oft-debated conclusion in his *Discourse on Method*, published in 1638. For Descartes, the answer to one of life's fundamental puzzles—proof of one's own existence—was a process of deduction and doubt. In other words, we can doubt whether our experiences are real, whether our conversations actually take place, even whether we are "here," wherever "here" might be. However, one *cannot* doubt, Descartes argued, that one, in fact, doubts. Thus, he concluded, "I think; therefore, I am,"—or more accurately, "I think; therefore I exist." I would go beyond this notion of Cartesian doubt to assert that philanthropy should cause us to assert, "We are; therefore, we must serve."

In closing, I offer a debt of gratitude to my friend Marybeth Gasman for asking me to participate in this great project. She is a fearless and tireless scholar who has made the decision to go where no woman (or man) has gone before *vis-à-vis* philanthropy among people of color, especially as concerns historically Black colleges and universities.

Finally, I would like to offer a word of gratitude to the person whom so many people hold in esteem as the "godfather" of African American development professionals, Charles Stephens. Friend, author, advocate, mentor—any single title is so inadequate as to be offensive. Charles has quietly encouraged and guided countless young people to great success in the field of fundraising. To borrow from a legendary British prime minister, "Never have so many owed so much to *one*." On behalf of those many, please accept my humble thank you.

Larry Smith
March 2011

Appendix 1: Author Perspectives

Why Philanthropy? Why Nonprofits?
Why Gender and Race?

In this chapter we discuss our own backgrounds and reasons for participating in the research and writing process of this book. Each of us was shaped by profound experiences as children, throughout our education and in our professional lives. By sharing these stories, we hope to encourage more research and writing in the area of race, gender, philanthropy, and nonprofit leadership.

Bigotry and Generosity: The Impetus for My Research

Marybeth Gasman

I grew up in a family of ten children in a very rural area of the Upper Peninsula of Michigan. We were horribly poor. I often tell people, "We were so poor that when my mom made chipped beef on toast, there wasn't any beef." My mom did the best she could on about $7,000 a year. People often ask how ten children and their parents could survive on so little money. The answer: we grew and made everything. As a child, I learned how to can fruits, make jams and jellies, wax vegetables for winter, cut sides of meat, gut fish and deer, and bake pies. Ironically, as an adult I do not eat meat.

Oftentimes our neighbors gave us clothes, fed us breakfast, and drove us places when our old car broke down. I wasn't embarrassed to receive this kind of help, because it just seemed normal to me. Everyone in our neighborhood helped one another. People sometimes even helped those they did not like as we were interdependent in many ways.

As children, we entertained ourselves. We did not have a television or any fancy games; we made up games. We climbed apple trees and shook them for fun, flooded the backyard to make an ice rink during winter, played "kick the can," and rode the tractor for sport. I remember making homes for my blond, bikini-clad Barbies out of old record albums and tape. My little sister and I entertained each other for hours with these makeshift Barbie homes.

We had no idea that we were poor. Of course our parents knew, but we kids thought that everyone lived this way. It was not until eighth grade, when our house burned to the ground and we had to live in temporary housing in a nearby small city, that we realized we were poor. I noticed what others had and the access that money—albeit not much—gave people. It was then that I discovered that I was on free lunch and that my school uniforms had been worn by my brothers and sisters before I wore them (it became a point of ridicule among kids at school). I wondered why my blouses were not white and why my tights had holes in the knees. I did not say much about my thoughts and feelings to anyone, because I knew it would hurt my mom and dad.

My mom was lovely, although she cried a lot. She tried her best to hide her tears, but her struggle was hard. My father was an adequate husband. Yet, he was resentful and jealous of others' accomplishments. He was bitter, and this emotion resulted in very little love shown toward my mother. Instead, he verbally abused her, labeling her stupid because of her lack of education. She did what she needed to raise her children and get through the madness that had her trapped in a life she had never envisioned. Perhaps what I admire most about my mom and why I am talking about her in an essay about philanthropy and nonprofit leadership is that she gave generously of herself while always speaking up and pushing back. In a provincial town, where many people conformed and took part in bigotry, my mom did not. She was accepting of everyone.

Sadly, my father was the opposite. When I wrote that he was bitter earlier, I was referring to his hatred of others, be they Blacks, Latinos, or Asians. Native Americans were spared for some reason (more than likely because my father was actually half American Indian). I grew up hearing my father say nigger, spic, Jap, and chink. But, I also grew up with a mother who told me that these words were wrong and hurtful. She washed our mouths out with soap if we ever repeated these words. I saw my older brothers endure the Zest or Dove bar many times. In my heart I knew those words were wrong and did not say them. My mom told us that hatred of someone on the basis of race, or color, or wealth was wrong. Of note, there were *no* African Americans, Latinos, or Asians living in our town or within 150 miles from us at any point during my childhood (and even today, the town has not changed much). But that didn't stop my father or many of the other residents of our town from hating these racial and ethnic groups. Oh, they were fun to laugh at on *Sanford and Son* and *Chico and the Man*, but you wouldn't want "those people" as friends. Minorities were easy targets.

My father did anything he could to convince us that African Americans were bad and that we should always hold them suspect. "Martin Luther King was a rabble rouser and didn't really believe in peaceful protest." "Malcolm X was anti-American." "Blacks were dirty and lazy; they just wanted a hand out." Ironically, my father was always trying to get government cheese, and he stole from his employer time and time again. Many of my school teachers reinforced these stereotypical, racist ideas. I learned nothing about African American history and culture with the exception of slavery (and that was whisked over and romanticized, and of course, there was no blame to be had). I heard teachers say derogatory things about Blacks. My Catholic grade school had a slave auction and was not apologetic about it. As a small child, I didn't see a problem with the slave auction. I didn't even know what slavery was, let alone the horrors of Jim Crow. Our local coffee shop was called "Little Black Sambos" and had a young African boy being chased by a tiger on the sign and on the menus. I thought Sambo was cute. The local bakery had big fat cookie jars decorated like a Black woman. I dug my hand in for a cookie never thinking twice about the image on the jar. I went to "Sambos" and the bakery with my father; my mother never took me to these places.

As my mom saw my father's influence on her children, she worked to counter it—ever so patiently. She told us not to listen to him. She confided in us—telling us how my dad blamed minorities for his lack of success, for his problems. She told us that she had grown up in Flint, Michigan, living next door to a Black family, and that they were "just like you and me." When she married my father she had no idea that he held such racist views. Many times these views do not surface for years, and by that time she had too many kids to make it on her own. She felt trapped. And as a result, she endured his hostile and shameful verbiage. Through our mother, some of us learned that prejudice is wrong and that we should speak up for others and confront injustice. Unfortunately, not all of my siblings learned this lesson—some of them harbor horrible thoughts and school their children in racist ideas. I no longer speak to these siblings—a choice I had to make when I had my own child.

Because of my mother, despite growing up in a racist and exclusionary environment, I chose to pursue a research agenda and scholarly life dedicated to issues of race. It makes sense to my mother. My father couldn't understand until very late in his life why his daughter would care so much about equity. In the spirit of true irony, my father had a stroke, and we placed him in a nursing home near my sister in Tennessee. Unlike the Upper Peninsula of Michigan, there are African Americans in Tennessee, and my father's roommate in the nursing home (he had a roommate because he could not afford a private room) was an African American man. Although disgusted and belligerent about the idea at first, my father grew to love the man and the man's family. They became close friends, and when I would visit him, the two of them would be sitting in rocking chairs laughing and sharing stories. A few months before my father died, he told me that he had been wrong about Blacks. He cried in my arms about the life of anger and hatred he had lived for over 80 years; he was proud of me for standing up against his racist beliefs. Sadly, he never acknowledged the work of my mother—a poor, abused, White woman who could have grown bitter—to push back against his influence over her children; he continued to resent her.

Given the example of my mother (and my father for that matter), my interest in race and equity might make sense. Despite not knowing anyone of another race or ethnicity (outside of Native Americans) until graduate school, I felt compelled to make a difference in the world. I idealistically believed (and still believe) that we should "be the change we want to see." I make no apologies for having this perspective. Yes, it might color my viewpoint—it might make a difference in what I choose to research. But it does not mean that I will cover up findings to appease my ideology. It does not mean that I'll avoid asking questions that run counter to my hopes. I believe that it is entirely possible to pursue a research agenda steeped in a commitment to justice.

Working in Nonprofit Environments

Much of my research pertains to philanthropy in communities of color and among African Americans specifically. I have also explored gender issues as they pertain to philanthropy. My interest in philanthropy and race stem from my upbringing, but they are also linked to my work in nonprofit environments.

My first encounter with the nonprofit world came when I was in college. I secured an internship at the YMCA in Green Bay, Wisconsin. Although I learned a few skills while working at the Y, the population it served was fairly homogeneous and the facility served more as an athletic club than a social service organization. I remember wondering why the entrance fees were so expensive given the historic mission of the Y. It seemed to be—keep in mind that I was only about 19—that the YMCA served White businessmen more than it reached out to the surrounding community.

I did not enter another nonprofit organization's walls until 1997, when I began a position raising money and directing several mentoring programs at the Ella Austin Community Center in San

Antonio, Texas. The Ella Austin Community Center has a long history of serving the surrounding African American community. It is located in a deeply impoverished area—one in which the houses have bars on the windows and sometimes worse; I once visited a home with refrigerators forming a bullet-proof vest around it. Still, the children in the area were filled with energy and joy and the Community Center reached out to them and provided a place of refuge.

Working at the Ella Austin Community Center was one of the most rewarding experiences of my life. I was the only White employee among 100 Black and Latino staff members. Regardless, I was welcomed into the Ella Austin family. I experienced immense giving, hard work, and a compassion for serving others that I had not seen before—with the exception of my mother. My supervisor, a 60-year-old African American man named Tony Hargrove with high-level military experience, taught me everything he knew about working with nonprofit boards, fundraising, caring for people in poor communities, and expressing dignity and humility.

Tony was there when I had my daughter Chloe. In fact he was the first person to hold her aside from my husband and me. From Tony, I learned how important a sense of empathy is when doing the work of a nonprofit.

Working at the Ella Austin Community Center pushed me in many ways. Much of what I thought about the world was challenged by the people I met and the lives they lived. I remember an incident in which an African American mother came to talk to me about acquiring financial assistance to help pay for her bills. To give her the money, I had to visit her home. When I pulled up to her home, I saw a satellite dish fastened to the outside of her house. I thought to myself, "Why does she need financial assistance if she can afford a satellite dish? I don't even have a satellite dish?" During my conversation with the mother, I asked her about the satellite dish, and she said, "Having a satellite dish guarantees that the kids hang out at my home. I always know they are safe." I was so mad at myself for my assumptions and judgments. That simple interaction made me much more sensitive to the struggles of the poor. In addition, it has forced me to think more deeply when I encounter new situation and to look for the things that are not so obvious. The interaction also helped me to think more deeply about African American philanthropy. For the most part, to study philanthropy in Black communities means that you have to look closely and keep an open mind. Oftentimes, philanthropy has a different appearance in low-income African American communities. People don't take credit for their giving as it is just a natural part of life. And, as a result, African Americans are left out of more mainstream assessments of philanthropy, such as Giving USA's assessment of giving.

Working with the Foundation Community

In 2000, I became a professor. Yes, I was still working for a nonprofit, but colleges and universities operate differently from small nonprofits. Because most of my work is related to fundraising, philanthropy, and communities of color, I have worked closely with the foundation community. This experience has been interesting in that I do research on the influence of foundations on minority institutions, but I also interact with their program officers and presidents. In many ways, I feel that I am living in my research. As I do this, I continually think about the ethical dimensions of the work I am doing. Are the foundations listening to the voice of those in communities of color? What role do people of color play in the foundation? Are foundations dictating an agenda or engaging the perspectives of people of color?

Most recently, I began working as a consultant and research advisor for a group of roughly 25 foundations that are interested in minority-serving institutions (MSIs). In this role, I advise the foundations on their work with MSIs and educate them on the many strengths and challenges that these institutions face. For me this work is wonderfully rewarding. It brings together my interest in philanthropy with my interest in MSIs. Yet, I constantly question the agenda of the foundations. I make sure that they listen to the voice of the MSI leaders and that these voices are central to the discussions among the foundation leaders. Of note, the program officers of most foundations have changed in color in recent years. Many of them are younger, people of color. This change in the racial makeup of foundation staff makes a significant difference in the work of foundations and helps to ensure that communities of color are listened to.

Coming Together

All of my experiences—those as a child, those working at nonprofits, and those working with foundations—have shaped my views on research and practice. And each of these experiences shaped the nature of this book. The combination of a racist father, a strong and giving mother, and the witnessing of profound generosity and empathy led to my interest in the topics in this book. I have deep admiration for the leaders featured and am dedicated to fostering opportunities for more individuals interested in leading in this way.

∼

From Crisp Dollar Bills to Inspirational Donor Stories: Why I Study Philanthropy

Noah D. Drezner

Friday mornings began with me getting dressed in blue pants, a white shirt, a clip-on tie, and my mother giving me what I remember as the most crisp dollar bill. It was so crisp that it could have just been printed. This is one of my clearest and only remaining memories of my mother, who passed away when I was in elementary school. That dollar bill was for *tzedakah*.

This memory is what sent me down a path to become a development officer and now a philanthropy scholar. Throughout my childhood, giving was part of the ethos; whether it was giving that crisp dollar bill, collecting the clothes that I grew out of for Good Will, doing different service projects, or helping my father and grandmother choose different organizations to write checks to at the end of the year, philanthropy—all though it was never called that—was always a part of my life.

The Hebrew word *tzedakah* is commonly translated as "charity." However, this is not the best translation. *Tzedakah* comes from the root *tzedek*, which means righteousness or justice. One of my favorite verses of the Torah is "*Tzedek, tzedek* you shall pursue in order to live," or "Justice, justice you shall pursue in order to live" (Deuteronomy 16:20). The connection between *tzedakah* and justice is not lost on me. I see one true power of philanthropy to create a more just world and a means to pursue social justice.

As a researcher I am aware that while philanthropy has the power to lead to social justice, it also has the means to maintain the status quo, only temporarily alleviating issues, or reinforcing existing power dynamics between the wealthy and lower socioeconomic classes. When thinking about theses different paradigms and critiques, I am often reminded of Martin Luther King Jr.'s writings from his 1963 book *Strength to Love:* "Philanthropy is commendable, but it must not cause the philanthropist to overlook the circumstances of economic injustice which make philanthropy necessary."

These beliefs and interests motivated me to pursue a career that explores and critiques philanthropy and why others engage in prosocial behavior.

There is no question that giving benefits both those receiving the gift and those donating it. Maya Angelou once said that she "found that among its other benefits, giving liberates the soul of the giver." The scholarly literature gives many reasons why people are motivated to give of their time and their wealth. There are extrinsic reasons, such as the recognition, entrée into social circles, tax benefits, and intrinsic reasons, such as paying forward the help of others, meeting religious obligations, and wanting to help others. The one that speaks most personally to me is what Andreoni (1989) calls the "warm glow." The warm glow refers to the feeling that donors might get when they help someone else.

For me that study of philanthropy and having a better understanding of the phenomenon of why people choose to act in a prosocial manner are important. In a society where people are born with different levels of privilege and therefore access, I believe that philanthropy can help those with less access gain a little more of a level playing field in their lives. This is not to say that philanthropy is just for the "haves" to give to the "have-nots." On the contrary, I believe that philanthropy is possible—and occurs—at all socioeconomic levels and takes many forms.

I choose to focus most of my work on philanthropy in communities that are not typically thought of as generous or philanthropic. However, they are! I have looked at communities of color, the deaf, and young adults.

My interest in these communities stems from my time as fundraiser at a small private research extensive institution. As a development officer I realized that we were almost exclusively engaging the White alumni in our fundraising. This frustrated me; why weren't we engaging our alumni of color, and why weren't they giving in response to the solicitations that they received?

When I asked questions of my senior colleagues, their answers were not sufficient. Therefore, I decided to return to graduate school to explore philanthropy and fundraising within a higher education context. As I read more, engaged in conversations, and began research, I realized that the reason we were not effective was that we were not asking in a culturally sensitive way. And, as we all know, if someone is not asked to give, he or she more than likely will not give.

Giving is a very personal thing. What motivates one person might not be compelling to others. What most interested me as a development officer and now interests me as a researcher is the personal stories of individual philanthropist—those who give of themselves at all levels—and why they are compelled to do the work that they do.

When working as a development officer, I was always interested in the stories about why people gave. Understanding their motivations made me more successful in aligning their priorities with those of the institution. Some were simple, giving because they were on scholarship as a student and felt a need to give back. Others were more complex, wanting to give to a specific program to address an issue on campus that negatively affected their student experience and the donor wanting to make sure that current and future students did not have the same experiences at their alma mater.

Recently, I was at a university campaign planning retreat. While there, I was in a session where donors and volunteers spoke about their motivations for giving the university. People rose and spoke from the heart. One trustee—a larger-than-life personality—whom I have known for nearly 15 years, spoke about her decision to make a campaign gift to endow and name the university's career and internship center. She spoke about how she would not have been able to attend the university as a child of a single mother without scholarships and would not have ended up on Wall Street if not for her summer internships and help from the career center when she was a student. The trustee continued that she was regularly approached by students and young alumni from the university for career advice, internships, and jobs in the financial sector. She then mentioned that she happily helps all university students; however, she asks in exchange all of them to make a gift to the university's Annual Fund and remain involved in university alumni activities. Her motivation to give was based on her experiences, yet her giving extends beyond dollars. She is motivated to increase participation and university involvement to enhance future students' experiences and give young alumni an additional experience of potentially having an impact on future students in a way that the alumni might not have received without working with this trustee. It is hearing stories like these that inspires me personally as a donor and as a researcher.

Within the context of our book, we look at female and foundation leaders of color and why they chose and what influenced their careers. It is clear that many of these leaders have chosen careers in which they are forgoing earnings. Simply, if they did other work, they would likely be drawing a higher salary. Why do people choose to do this? A similar question was the basis of my first academic publication, "Thurgood Marshall: A Study of Philanthropy through Racial Uplift," in Marybeth Gasman and Katherine V. Sedgwick's *Uplifting a People: Essays on African American Philanthropy In Education* (Peter Lang, 2005). In both cases, the influence of others in their family and the belief in the cause influence the leaders' decisions.

As with many of the participants in this book's study and in others, it is clear from my experience that the influence of others, most notably my family, and my relationship with Judaism, and religion in general, effected my decisions to both give and make my career choices.

Recently, while attending a Unitarian Universalist religious service to commemorate the hundredth anniversary of the passing of the Black abolitionist and suffragist Frances Ellen Watkins Harper, the congregation was asked to recite the Stewardship Testimonial written by Janice Tosto.

> We pick fruit from trees we did not plant. We drink water from wells we did not dig. This is as it should be so long as we dig and plant for those who come after.

These three short sentences sum up my continued commitment to philanthropy. This testimonial speaks to the fact that we are all recipients of others' generosity. Even the most privileged and wealthy members of society benefit from the prosocial behaviors and philanthropy of others.

At a time where political discourse in the United States is focused on the individual rather than the collective, I believe that this is an important reminder about how all of us benefit from the actions of others. Philanthropy is one means—across all cultures, races, ethnicities, and religions—in which community is built upon.

For my own personal philanthropic goals, I would only add to the testimonial that we should not only replace what we eat and drink but make sure that there is even more to sustain future generations.

These personal goals and my life experiences from childhood on had a profound influence on the framing of all of work that I have done as a practitioner turned scholar.

∼

Labeling Race, Ethnicity, and Gender in the Nonprofit World

Edward Epstein

My experience as a White male working in arts and education-based nonprofits has allowed me to observe from a unique vantage point the challenges faced by minority nonprofit leaders. As the product of an affluent suburb, I grew up with plenty of opportunities for education and advancement—but little exposure to people from other races and backgrounds. As a child, I imagined that others' experience resembled my own—that with the right combination of luck and hard work, the same doors should be open to anyone.

This view changed very little until I found myself in the midst of urban dystopia. Having chosen art as my field, I headed for the city after graduation. Living at first in Chicago, and later in San Antonio, Atlanta, and Philadelphia, I began to meet individuals who had grown up in very different circumstances from those I had experienced.

Arriving in Philadelphia in 2003, I embarked on a collaboration to create art studios in an unused building owned by the University of Pennsylvania. This put me in the thick of a decades-old conflict between town and gown, in which local residents had seen their neighborhood shrink while their Ivy League neighbor expanded. Memories of land grabs created an atmosphere of distrust between local activists and university representatives. When they bore the Penn label, even well-intentioned efforts to improve the quality of life were greeted with skepticism.

It was in this charged atmosphere that I discovered a new calling, that of community leader in the arts. So that my studio space would not be regarded as a foreign invasion—an effort to move artists in and locals out—I began by asking neighborhood leaders for input on how to run the new arts program. These leaders, along with Penn professors, would select artists for the studios. It was decided that spaces should be offered to neighborhood residents at no charge in exchange for service to the community. Artists would also be provided a gallery in which to show their work. But which community members would receive this generous offer?

The selection process was a delicate dance around the tensions between town and gown, minority and White, local culture and international. People talked about the need to have artists with the "right" background but without ever using the words "Black," "Latino," "minority," or "artist of color." A dispute about how much to count the quality of an artist's work versus the suitability of their background was really about how many minority artists to pick. How did the program find minority artists? In the absence of a race label on the application, the selection panel scanned the resumes and the work intently for clues: a person grew up on such-and-such street, showed his or her work in a certain gallery, belonged to a certain organization, had certain references in his or her work. Above all, it was assumed that local Black and Latino leaders would nominate their own candidates for the program.

It was in this context that I began to understand the many unusual expectations placed on minority artists and cultural leaders. Whatever their individual accomplishments, minority artists were often shunted into well-defined categories that fit panelists' expectations. Minority leaders were expected to aid in this process, bringing the "right kind" of candidates up for consideration and applying a gloss that helped others to interpret their work. For example, Black or Latino artists who never had an opportunity to study could operate in the "outsider" category. These artists were permitted to submit poorly produced work samples and incomplete applications—deficiencies that were deemed part of their authenticity. Those minority artists who were academically trained, on the other hand, were expected to be *better prepared* than their White counterparts. Many of them were: they had put in extra effort to succeed in an art school system that assumed that they lacked the skills to succeed. Another group fit the category of "race conscious" or overtly political artist. Where overt politics might be seen as uncouth among White artists, they seemed to fit perfectly well within White panelists' views of what a minority artist should be.

Reinforcing these rigid categories were grant-making institutions and ultimately audiences. Foundations and government agencies needed to show that they were distributing funds to the underfunded. How could they tell that they were reaching that goal? Categories provided an easy expedient. A certain kind of minority artist, for example, could be counted on to bring "neighborhood folks" into the gallery on the opening night. For the organization applying for a grant, listing that artist on a grant application was shorthand for audience diversity. Audiences were promised a show that spoke to them; nonprofit leaders knew that these artists would give their organization the right amount of "color;" and grant makers knew that their dollars were reaching the right people.

More recently, as the community engagement specialist in a performing arts center, I discovered the same forces at work in other artistic media. Designations like "Roots Series" connoted art suitable for minority audiences—jazz, blues, and gospel, for example. Such performances were marketed heavily among minorities and touted to the foundations wishing to know that that the theater offered a diverse lineup of artists. This situation was not all bad—sometimes the performers brought in under the "Roots" rubric were quite good and offered a welcome relief to stodgy fare in the regular season. However, the fact remained that "Roots" performers were less free to break out of their particular genre.

Seeing the forces of categorization in action has helped me to understand the dilemmas faced by my minority colleagues throughout the nonprofit world. It is on this basis that I offer my contributions to *Race, Gender, and Leadership in Nonprofit Organizations* Stories told by individuals such as Emmett Carson and Kanyere Eaton about how the roles they had been expected to play during the course of their careers sounded familiar. I knew from my own experience that Black, Latino, and female leaders were often made to feel that they should represent their own kind in a certain way. I knew also about the code language that was used to discuss race in the nonprofit world—a place where people were supposedly committed to discussing race problems openly.

As in the exchanges I had witnessed in the artist-in-residence program, racism was not outward but subtle. It consisted in the fact of minority contributors not being allowed to define their own niche, but instead being forced to accept one that was convenient for the majority. It was sad but not surprising to hear that such situations also existed for participants in social service nonprofits, and in the highest echelons of academe.

I was interested to hear about how minority leaders maintained their commitment to nonprofit work and held on to their values in spite of the pressures and ambiguities that they faced. These leaders recognized how much they had to offer by being a minority role model in a leadership position—yet they knew that they would have to fight to be more than a figurehead. As Emmett Carson pointed out, there were many in the establishment for whom having a minority in a key position was enough, and to actually listen to what they had to say was going too far. My own experience in the nonprofit world has helped me to admire the leadership of Carson and others who have chosen to make a statement, not just by being there but by changing the rules of the game. Their resistance offered hope that someday the nonprofit world will truly represent the aspirations of all who seek to build a better world.

$\sim$

How I Came to This Work

Tyrone Freeman

Research on philanthropy is often conceptualized as the voluntary action that occurs in a sector distinct from the market (private sector) and the state (public sector), and often referred to as "nonprofit," "independent," "philanthropic," or "third." Debates and models abound as to how many sectors there are, what to call them, and how they relate to one another. Among them are arguments for the inclusion of a fourth sector defined as the family or household. Van Til (1988) argued for adding the household or informal sector to the three-sector model to account for the role of families and neighborhoods in generating material and nonmaterial resources for the other three sectors. Smith (1991) expanded upon this by defining the household sector as not only those living together but also those engaged in mutual and informal helping and caring behaviors regardless of residence. This would include family members, friends, neighbors, and even co-workers. Additionally, in describing civil society, O'Connell (1999) presented a visual model that layered the traditional three sectors on top of a foundation that included the individual and the community.

Whether it is recognized as a formal sector or not, the family/household provides important values and resources that enable the other sectors to operate, such as money, votes, labor, and energy. In the case of the nonprofit sector, the family/household provides the values and moral commitments that inform the sector's expressive dimensions, and this is clearly evident in our text. The subjects in this study were deeply influenced by their upbringing in particular families and particular communities during particular times that shared, taught, and promoted values such as faith, justice, equality, education, fairness, and perseverance. Indeed, it is highly evident that the home and community backgrounds of the subjects influenced their psychosocial development as individuals and shaped their commitments and careers as leaders in philanthropy. Regardless of race, generation, gender, or geography, I can relate to their stories.

I was raised in a religious African American family in a middle-class, suburban community in northern New Jersey. We had extended family and community networks that espoused an ethos of caring, sharing, and uplift. As the son, grandson, nephew, and cousin of Baptist preachers, I watched the men in my family "talk the talk" from pulpits on Sunday mornings and my entire family—men and women—"walk the walk" through service and sacrifice the other six days of the week at home, on the job, and in the community. Priorities were clear: (1) God, (2) family, (3) education, and (4) community. Just like many of the leaders in this study, I, too, had high expectations for my own academic performance, personal character, and spiritual development. "C" grades were not acceptable, and respect, truth, reverence, and responsibility were demanded. Supportive communities surrounded and nurtured me, informing me of who I was and what I was capable of achieving. I remember vividly when as a teenager, a member of my home church stopped me one Sunday morning after service and said simply and directly, "You could be president of the United States if you want to." He then patted me on my back and walked away smiling. He has since passed away and could never have even dreamed about Barack Obama, but he did not need to because he spoke his dreams and aspirations into my generation and fueled our pursuit of excellence and possibilities.

The leaders in this study were also deeply influenced by historical moments that punctuated their lives and framed their existence, whether in navigating the constraints of Jim Crow segregation or breaking through racial and gender barriers in the social movements of the sixties. My career is still in process, but I also share a historical sensibility. The historian Joyce Appleby has written an extraordinary text about a generation she calls the first Americans, those born immediately after the revolutionary era and founding of the United States, thus earning them rightful claim to the moniker. In similar fashion, I have wrestled with the idea of my generation, those born in the seventies or after the Civil Rights Movement as the first "African Americans"—that is, the first generation of African Americans who did not experience legalized oppression; whose humanity and citizenship were fully acknowledged and protected under federal, state, and local laws without qualification; and who were therefore perhaps better positioned to participate and contribute to American society than any other previous generation of African Americans. It's not as perfect a claim as Appleby's, because inequities persist and disparities abound. But the idea is interesting nonetheless because I certainly have had opportunities that my grandfathers could never have conceived. Simultaneously, I recognize that many in my generation still struggle, and the pursuit of opportunity and justice continues.

Supportive educational environments were critical to the leaders in this study, and to me. As the current debate about public school reform rages, I feel blessed to have been educated in a fine public educational system in New Jersey that had high graduation rates and rates of college attendance and completion across races and genders. I vividly recall many educators who helped me in numerous ways and were White, Black, male and female. A few of the leaders in this study acknowledged both the educational barriers and supports that guidance counselors provided. My high school guidance counselor was an African American woman who demanded and expected much of me and guided me to pre-college experiences and opportunities that further facilitated my entry into college and launching as an independent individual. I remain indebted to her and frequently recall her influence and that of the other handful of African American counselors and teachers who also worked in my school and cared for all students, but particularly the Black students. My educational support system continued at Lincoln University of the Commonwealth of Pennsylvania, a historically Black university, which nurtured my development. Several leaders in the study attended historically Black colleges and universities (HBCUs) and recalled the influence of those environments. I cannot begin to express the power and motivation I experienced on Lincoln's campus surrounded by African American, Asian, and African Ph.D.'s from across the disciplines—literary critics, physicists, psychologists, chemists, sociologists. They knew their fields, and they were intent upon helping us as students not only learn those fields but also catch a glimpse of who we could become and relentlessly pursue those dreams. I was also aided tremendously by a White female English professor who encouraged and challenged my writing abilities and gave me my first two opportunities to present papers at academic conferences while still an undergraduate. And so I laugh at the many HBCU "haters" who have never set foot on any campus, are blinded by their biases and double standards, and have no clue about the true work and effectiveness of HBCUs.

And, finally, I, too, come from a family and community that believed in and lived philanthropy—although we never used the term or even conceptualized what we did in such a manner. It was a way of life to help those in need whether they were family members or not. I have another childhood memory of being in New Orleans with my family attending a religious conference. As we packed our bags and prepared to check out of our hotel, we had some food left over from our week-long stay, mainly fruits and other snacks. Instead of throwing the food away, my sister and I remembered a homeless man we frequently saw during our time in the city who camped out on the sidewalk a couple blocks from the hotel. We asked our parents if we could give the food to him. It was a natural thought that emerged from the example of Christ taught in our home and that my parents set of caring for many in our family, neighborhood, church, and community networks. My parents gladly walked us down the street to find the man, and we gave him the food and they also gave him some money. Today, my father's ministry of meeting people's spiritual and human needs continues, as does my mother's particular talent and commitment of caring for senior citizens and meeting their health, transportation, and emotional needs for companionship and love.

So, my family of origin and experiences as an African American male have a lot to do with why and how I came to this work. But I also came to this work from at least two other perspectives: a nonprofit practitioner and a scholar of philanthropy. My practitioner perspective is grounded in nearly 15 years of experience as a professional fundraiser serving a variety of organizational missions, including community development, youth and family social services, and higher education. I've worked in local community-based organizations and a Big Ten public university system, all in the Midwest. My current work in the field includes teaching and developing curricula to support the continuing education and professional development needs of fundraising professionals and nonprofit managers in the United States and abroad. My scholarly perspective is influenced by graduate studies in urban community development and adult education, and doctoral work in philanthropic studies and higher education. My research has focused on the history of philanthropy, philanthropy and higher education, and African American philanthropy, in particular its historical evolution and diverse expressions. My experience as a practitioner provides a lens through which

I view much of my work as a scholar. My work as a scholar is informed by burning questions and concerns that emerged from my own social and cultural experiences as an African American male. So when Marybeth invited me to join this research project, my immediate answer was yes.

I answered in the affirmative because I have had the experience of being the only African American fundraiser in professional meetings. I have seen the shock on the faces of donors who did not think the voice over the phone matched the face they were meeting for the first time. I know that there are several people who do not expect me to be a fundraiser or a scholar. Similarly, there are still prevalent myths that hold that African Americans are recipients of philanthropy and not agents of it, and that women do nothing meaningful in philanthropy besides cute "volunteer" work. So, I know that race and gender still matter. As American society becomes increasingly more diverse in many ways, it is imperative that we understand the experiences of different people in our field of philanthropy. The mainstream narrative and experience no longer captures the complexity, beauty, and opportunity of our historical moment (and it never has). Women and people of color have historically made tremendous contributions to philanthropy, and they continue to today as well. We must continue to study and disseminate their stories and integrate them into the mainstream narrative and make space for the entry of more to join the ranks. In many ways, the strength of our democracy depends upon this happening.

I happen to live in a community that has a significant cadre of African American and women foundation leaders whose presence and various moral commitments have greatly impacted the fabric of local community life for the better because of the perspectives, voices, and sense of responsibility they bring to the tables where important decisions are made. This book is an attempt to shed light on who such people are and how they came to their positions so we may know how to broaden and clear that path so more may come. I am honored to have contributed to it.

$\sim$

Reasons for Research

Vida L. Avery

Coauthoring this book made me reflect on how and why I moved into the philanthropic sector. I became interested in changing my career to the philanthropic arena when I focused on nineteenth-century philanthropists and their impact on Black higher education for my doctoral dissertation. Because scholars had not discussed my topic in detail, The Creation of the Atlanta University Systems (1929), I spent a great deal of time researching and reading through primary documents (mostly letters) left behind by men such as John D. Rockefeller Sr. and Andrew Carnegie. It was fascinating to grasp how their upbringing, education (or the lack thereof), religion, and life experiences shaped their worldview and were part of the impetus behind their philanthropy and the creation of foundations.

As an African American woman who is a fourth-generation educator and a graduate of Spelman College, I knew I directly benefitted from these men's philanthropy, particularly the Rockefeller family, as did several members of my family. Although I was familiar with some of Rockefeller's involvement with Spelman, through my research I learned of the innerworkings behind the scene during the early 1900s that solidified the existence of the college, which has lasted now for 130 years. Without their effort (and others), I wondered if this would be the case. After completing my research and dissertation, I concluded three things: (1) the measure of these early philanthropists' lives rested far beyond the surface of what most literature revealed about them; (2) the impact of their philanthropic endeavors exists in society today; and (3) I wanted to change my career focus to this arena.

My first job was a program officer at a foundation in Texas. I must admit that in many ways it was a nontraditional foundation. Its capital was not monetary awards. We awarded technology (e.g., state-of-the-art laptop computers, printers, cameras) to schools and nonprofit organizations throughout the United States. Nevertheless, I learned the intricacies of the grant-making process from a funder's perspective—reviewing/scoring applications, vetting applicants, visiting sites, and preparing the information about the organizations that I wanted to move forward for the board docket. This experience also provided me with an insider's view of how decisions were made about which organizations received a grant. Although the board ultimately decided the awards, the program officers were the advocates for the organizations and selected the ones that moved forward.

Being nontraditional might also explain the foundation's diverse staff of program officers: men and women, numerous people of color with different ethnicities, religion, and sexual orientation. The makeup of the staff indeed reflected the majority of the people throughout the United States. We all had social capital with various perspectives and viewpoints when we discussed the applications. However, in stark contrast, no persons of color held the executive or board positions; they were all White and the majority male.

Out of curiosity, I began to research other foundations and nonprofits in Texas, the larger, "more traditional" ones, because I wanted to find out if our foundation's staff composite was the norm. Unfortunately, it was not. Most of the foundations or nonprofits lacked staff who reflected the diverse communities they served. This lack of diversity was not only reflected with underrepresented program officers, but also with the executive positions and board members. It became evident that there were exclusionary hiring practices in this sector and state.

Now, I have moved to the other side of the philanthropic sector, the fundraising arena. I work with nonprofit, faith- and community-based organizations by assisting them with their grant-related needs. While working in this capacity I have kept abreast of philanthropic news, trends, and topics discussed. A few years ago, I noticed several philanthropic journal articles that focused on diversity in nonprofits. However, most of the discussions were on a broad spectrum. Rarely did I read an article that discussed having interviewed executive leaders of foundations and nonprofits who were people of color.

What I did notice throughout my reading was that the fundraising arena and professional associations were making a concerted effort to make their membership more diverse and inclusive in a meaningful way. From starting as a regular member a few years ago to being on the board of the Association of Fundraising Professionals—Greater Houston Chapter (AFP-GHC) now, I have witnessed firsthand the impact of these efforts. Our chapter received the 2010 AFP Friends of Diversity Designation, a national award given to chapters that have accomplished many of the key objectives in advancing diversity strategic goals. One of the ways our chapter achieve this award was through our Youth in Philanthropy commitment, which falls under Community Outreach and Diversity. National AFP spearheaded this initiative to engage youth (under 25) to become involved and to consider the profession in philanthropy. As such, our chapter collaborated with the University of Houston's American Humanics (AH) program and students. In doing so, several members and I created activities and events for the students as a means of an introduction into the field (matched students with mentors, invited them to monthly luncheons, hosted students at our places of employment, etc.).

One event always stays in the forefront of my mind above the others: the panel discussions that the committee members had with the AH students. The panel generally consisted of four to five AFP-GHC members, male and female, but all of us are African American. The students were not surprised that we all had careers in fundraising. The surprise was that we were all African Americans with careers in fundraising. The revelation that we were at ease discussing race/ethnicity and even holding a session on donors of color quite naturally led to an in-depth discussion of diversity in the nonprofit sector—which in the end, the students greatly appreciated. Though we have a long way to go in fully embracing the diversity on our board and within our membership, as do other chapters, we are moving in the right direction by having meaningful discussions about diversity.

Suffice it to say, when Marybeth Gasman asked me to be a coauthor of a book that focused on African American leaders of foundations and nonprofits, I was honored and elated to join the team. I knew from my own experience as a program officer that race and gender played a vital role in how I viewed potential grantees, their programs, and the communities they served. I also knew that this book would be unique. Having the interviews as a starting point meant that we were creating a different way to discuss diversity by using a different lens from which to view it.

This book will provide the reader with not only an avenue into the mindset of these leaders, but also an insight into their activism. Just as I was intrigued when I read the nineteenth-century philanthropists' letters, backstories, some of their motives for giving, and their formalizing the world of philanthropy as we know it today, my interest was equally piqued with this book. I wanted the opportunity to read the transcripts and learn what path led these leaders into the nonprofit arena. Accordingly, this book will also be a good reference for individuals who are new to the field.

Most important, telling stories or highlighting people and topics in a manner that goes beneath the surface has always been an interest of mine. If not for this book, the stories of these leaders and their level of accomplishments probably would never be told, especially not in the collective, thematic manner in which we have done. In doing so, I hope that this book will bridge the gap and add pertinent information to the literature on diversity and inclusiveness in the nonprofit arena.

Appendix 2: Diversity in Leadership Resource Supplement

Many of the leaders featured in this book benefited from various leadership and educational opportunities pertaining to empowering female and minority leaders; others did not. We have included herein a list of resources throughout the country for nonprofit and foundation leaders. We hope they are useful.

Nonprofit Leadership Initiatives

Academy for Educational Development (Washington, DC)
www.cld.aed.org

The Academy for Educational Development strives to facilitate effective leadership at all levels of society. It has a solid record of advancing opportunity, equity, and inclusion to ensure that the leadership of the future has a major impact and is diverse in all respects.

Alaska Humanities Forum (Anchorage, AK)
www.akhf.org/programs/leadership/leadership_main.html

Leadership Anchorage strives to provide a "full experience" in leadership training. Diverse participants build a network of peers, are nurtured through a mentor relationship that often continues beyond the program, prepare and implement a community service project, and apply their leadership training throughout the program. Participants emerge from the program prepared to fill leadership roles, filled with the desire to tackle a diverse array of community problems and challenges. The program seeks to ensure that the leadership of the city of Anchorage represents all of its citizens.

Alliance for Nonprofit Management (San Francisco, CA)
www.allianceonline.org/content/index.php?pid=55

The Alliance for Nonprofit Management's Cultural Competency Initiative (CCI) is working in areas such as fundraising, strategic planning, and board development to ensure diversity. Participants gain skills through the CCI to help nonprofits advance diversity and multiculturalism in staff, boards, policies, programs, stakeholder engagement, and communities served.

Anthem (Indianapolis, IN)
www.anthem.com

The Academy is sponsored by Anthem Blue Cross and Blue Shield, which, in January, won Mayor Bart Peterson's top award for its diversity-related initiatives and commitment within the company, as well as the community. The Indianapolis Urban League also collaborates in the program, which was developed by the American Institute for Managing Diversity, the nation's foremost nonprofit dedicated to diversity management education and research.

Asia Society (New York, NY)
www.sites.asiasociety.org/diversityforum

Asia Society convenes CEOs, senior leaders, and decision makers from Fortune 500 companies to discuss best practices and cutting-edge issues related to leadership and career development; including managing a globally diverse workforce in the United States and Asia and cultural fluency.

Association for Public Policy Analysis and Management
(Washington, DC)
www.appam.org/about/diversity.asp

The association has an active diversity committee that provides guidance on how to enhance diverse participation within the association. Initiatives include recruiting researchers from various disciplines, encouraging the participation of women in the association's leadership, and engaging in outreach to minority-oriented social science affinity groups and associations to encourage participation in the association among researchers from minority backgrounds.

Cardinal Stritch University (Milwaukee, WI)
www.stritch.edu/Community_Ties/Leadership_Center/Latino_
  Leadership.aspx

The leadership center at Cardinal Stritch University fosters Latino leadership through the Hispanic Professionals of Greater Milwaukee and hosts an annual development conference for Latino professionals.

Center for Nonprofit Advancement (Washington, DC)
www.nonprofitadvancement.org/news/action-planning-
  diversifying-local-nonprofit-leadership

The Center for Nonprofit Advancement convenes meetings and produces reports on diversity among the region's nonprofits.

Diversity Leadership Alliance (Phoenix, AZ)
www.diversityleadershipalliance.org

Diversity Leadership Alliance (DLA) is a nonprofit organization that provides diversity and inclusion education, resources, tools, and forums to the Phoenix area.

Georgia Center for Nonprofit Leaders (Atlanta, GA)
www.gcn.org/learn/ExecutiveandLeadershipPrograms/
  HighPotentialDiverse Leaders.aspx

The Georgia Center for Nonprofit Leaders hosts a program titled High Potential Diverse Leaders. The program is designed to be an immersive and enriching experience of training, access, and interaction with nonprofit leaders and opportunities to develop their peer networks and support systems.

GoLead Nonprofits First (Palm Beach County, FL)

GoLead offers a wide choice of services and programs for leaders in the nonprofit community. From personal leadership development to entrepreneurship, from board development to board governance, and to consulting services, GoLead specializes in providing nonprofit leaders with the tools to support successful nonprofit management and ensure the delivery of well-managed services.

Heart of West Michigan United Way (Grand Rapids, MI)
hwmuwvc.org/content/project-blueprint
www.nonprofitsfirst.org/RisingLeaders

United Way's Project Blueprint is a leadership development program that aims to increase the number of professionals of color providing leadership in local health, government, and human services organizations. Project Blueprint training consists of four evening sessions plus a visit to a board meeting.

Human Rights Campaign (Washington, DC)

The Human Rights Campaign (HRC) Diversity & Inclusion Council was founded in 2008 to support the Human Rights Campaign's stated commitment to diversity and inclusion at every level of the organization. From professional diversity consultants to leading business executives, religious leaders, youth, advocates from the lesbian, gay, bisexual, and transgender community, and civil rights principals, the council consists of individuals who represent the broad tapestry of the communities in which we live and work.

Leadership Education for Asian Pacifics, Inc. (San Francisco, CA)
www.leap.org/develop_main.html

Through a comprehensive range of signature leadership development programs, workshops, and customized services designed by and for Asian and Pacific Islanders (APIs), LEAP develops and cultivates talented leaders for the educational, nonprofit, private, and public sectors.

Mel King Institute for Community Building (Boston, MA)
www.melkinginstitute.org/2009/09/initiative-for-diversity-in-civic-leadership

The Initiative for Diversity in Civic Leadership provides education and training opportunities to help individuals from diverse political backgrounds to successfully run for elected office, manage and run political campaigns, and serve in all levels of government.

National Hispana Leadership Institute (Arlington, VA)
www.nhli.org/empower_conference/nyc/index.html

The National Hispana Leadership Institute coordinates annual conference aimed at empowering Latinas in nonprofit positions.

National Multicultural Institute (Washington, DC)
www.nmci.org/leadership_institutes/

The institute hosts the Diversity Leadership Conference, which brings together leaders in the field of diversity and inclusion across nonprofits, national, state, and local governments, and corporations. Attendees are responsible for helping their organizations successfully navigate the multicultural landscape.

New Leadership Puget Sound (Seattle, WA)
www.depts.washington.edu/newlead/whyapply.htm

The organization hosts annual conferences for emerging female leaders.

Nonprofit Leadership Alliance (Kansas City, MO)
www.humanics.org/site/c.omL2KiN4LvH/b.2480105/k.1764/
    Initiative_for_Nonprofit_Sector_Careers.htm

The Nonprofit Leadership Alliance's initiative for nonprofit sector careers is a national campaign to recruit, prepare, and retain a skilled and diverse next-generation of nonprofit section leadership.

Office of Neighborhood Involvement (Portland, OR)
www.portlandonline.com/oni/index.cfm?c=45147

The Office of Neighborhood Involvement's Diversity and Civic Leadership initiative hosts meetings that were largely developed and advocated for by the Diversity and Civic Leadership Committee (DCLC). The DCLC is a grassroots community-based effort that includes representatives from underrepresented organizations, neighborhood district coalitions, and neighborhood associations.

San Jose Silicon Valley Chamber of Commerce (San Jose, CA)
www.sjchamber.com/about/education.php

The San Jose Silicon Valley Chamber of Commerce's Community Leadership San Jose Silicon Valley (CLSJSV) identifies people who are emerging leaders within the San Jose metropolitan area and offers them a broad range of exposure to issues vital to the community.

University of Chicago (Chicago, Ill)
www.uchicago.edu/diversity/workplace.shtml

The University of Chicago offers professional organizations for women and minorities diversity training courses and maintains an office of business diversity and community affairs to ensure that women- and minority-owned businesses are given a fair chance to conduct business with the university.

Executive Education in Nonprofit Leadership

University of Washington (http://evans.washington.edu/executive-education/cascade/ nonprofit-leadership-institute)

Stanford University (http://www.gsb.stanford.edu/exed/epnl/)

Harvard University (http://www.exed.hbs.edu/programs/spnm/Pages/default.aspx)

University of Pennsylvania (http://executiveeducation.wharton.upenn.edu/custom-programs/industry-practices/public-social-sectors/nonprofit-organizations-foundations/index.cfm)

Boston University (http://management.bu.edu/exec/elc/inml/index.shtml)

Columbia University (http://www4.gsb.columbia.edu/socialenterprise/alumni/ nonprofitboard)

Bryn Mawr College (http://www.brynmawr.edu/neli/)

Notre Dame University (http://business.nd.edu/executive_ education/integral_leadership_portfolio/eil/)

University of North Dakota (http://www.und.edu/dept/nlcp/)

University of Connecticut (http://continuingstudies.uconn.edu/professional/nonprofit/ index.html)

New York University (http://wagner.nyu.edu/leadership/leadership_dev/nonprofit_ programs.php)

The Center on Philanthropy at Indiana University (http://www. philanthropy.iupui.edu/TheFundRaisingSchool/Course Descriptions/certificatenonprofitexecutiveleadership.aspx)

Notes

Introduction

1. Francis Kunreuther for Annie E. Casey Foundation, Up Next: Generation Change and the Leadership of Nonprofit Organizations. Baltimore, MD: Annie E. Casey Foundation, 2005.
2. Census Bureau News U.S., "Texas Becomes Nation's Newest 'Majority Minority' State," August 11, 2005, www.census.gov, accessed September 24, 2009. In 2005, the U.S. Census Bureau identified Texas, Hawaii, New Mexico, and California as "majority-minority" states, with Maryland, Mississippi, Georgia, New York, and Arizona following with 40 percent of the states' population consisting of minorities. "Majority-minorities" is a term used to describe a state whose racial composition is less than 50 percent White. Minorities in this sense include Hispanics/Latinos, African Americans, Asian Americans, American Indians, and Alaska natives.
3. Marybeth Gasman and Katherine V. Sedgwick (Eds.), *Uplifting a People: African American Philanthropy and Education* (New York: Peter Lang, 2005).
4. Alice Ginsberg and Marybeth Gasman, *Gender and Educational Philanthropy: New Perspectives on Funding, Collaboration, and Assessment* (New York: Palgrave, 2007).
5. Bradford Smith, Sylvia Shue, Jennifer Lisa Vest and Joseph Villarreal, *Philanthropy in Communities of Color* (Bloomington, IN: Indiana University Press, 1999). See also a study conducted in 2000 by the W. K. Kellogg Foundation titled *Emerging Philanthropy in Communities of Color: A Report on Current Trends,* as well as the one conducted by the Council on Foundations titled *Cultures of Caring: Philanthropy and Diverse American Communities* (Washington, DC: Council on Foundations, 1999).

6. Janice Gow Pettey, *Cultivating Diversity in Fundraising* (San Francisco: Wiley & Sons, 2002).
7. Mary Ellen S. Capek and Molly Mead, *Effective Philanthropy: Organizational Success through Deep Diversity and Gender Equality*, a Project of Women & Philanthropy funded by the W. K. Kellogg Foundation (Cambridge, MA: The MIT Press, 2006).
8. Sandra C. Shaw and Martha A. Taylor, *Reinventing Fundraising: Realizing the Potential of Women's Philanthropy* (San Francisco: Jossey-Bass, 1995).
9. The Center for Effective Philanthropy, "Assessment to Action: Creating Change," a Report on a Gathering of Foundation CEOs, Trustees, and Senior Executives, 2007, http://www.effectivephilanthropy.org/images/pdfs/CEP_Assessment_to_Action_Conference_Pub_2007.pdf, accessed September 16, 2009; Judith A. Ross, "Aligning for Impact: Connecting the Dots," The Center for Effective Philanthropy, 2009, http://www.effectivephilanthropy.org/images/pdfs/CEP_2009_Conference_Publication.pdf, accessed September 16, 2009; Rockefeller Philanthropy Advisors, "Diversity & Inclusion: Lessons from the Field," and the Council on Foundations, 2008, http://rockpa.org/wp-content/uploads/2008/12/diversity-inclusion.pdf, accessed October 1, 2009; Katherine Pease & Associates, "Inside Inclusiveness: Race, Ethnicity and Nonprofit Organizations," The Denver Foundation, 2003, http://www.nonprofitinclusiveness.org/files/Inside_Inclusiveness_Full_Report_0.pdf, accessed October 5, 2009; Jessica Chao, Julia Parshall, Desiree Amador, Meghna Shah and Armando Yanez, "Philanthropy in a Changing Society: Achieving Effectiveness through Diversity," Rockefeller Philanthropy Advisors, 2008, www.rockpa.org/ideas_and_perspectives/publications, accessed October 1, 2009; Kevin Bolduc et al., "Beyond the Rhetoric: Foundation Strategy," The Center for Effective Philanthropy, 2007, http://www.effectivephilanthropy.org/images/pdfs/CEP_Beyond_the_Rhetoric.pdf, accessed September 16, 2009; Lynn Burbridge et al., "The Meaning and Impact of Board and Staff Diversity in the Philanthropic Field," Foreward by Emmett D. Carson, Joint Affinity Groups, Minneapolis, MN: The University of Minnesota, 2002, http://www.mcf.org/Mcf/resource/JAGreport.htm, accessed September 29, 2009. This list is only a sample and is not exhaustive.

10. Marla Cornelius, Patrick Corvington and Albert Ruesga, "Ready to Lead: Next Generation Leaders Speak Out" (Baltimore, MD: CompassPoint Nonprofit Services, The Annie E. Casey Foundation & Meyer foundation, 2008), 16–20.

11. Council on Foundations, *Cultures of Caring: Philanthropy in Diverse American Communities* (Washington, DC: Council on Foundations, 1999).

Chapter 1

1. Ella L. J. Edmondson and S. M. Nkomo, *Our Separate Ways: Black and White Women and the Struggle for Professional Identity* (Boston, MA: Harvard Business School Press, 2001).

Chapter 2

1. Gara La Marche, "Taking Account of Race: A Philanthropic Imperative," Waldemar Nielsen Issue Forums in Philanthropy, Georgetown University for Public and Nonprofit Leadership, Georgetown Public Policy Institute, http://atlanticphilanthropies. org/news, accessed October 18, 2009.

2. Kathleen Bennett deMarrais and Margaret D. LeCompte, *The Way Schools Work: A Sociological Analysis of Education*, 3rd ed. (New York, NY: Addison Wesley Longman, Inc, 1999), 258.

3. Ian F. Hanley Lopez, "The Social Construction of Race: Some Observation on Illusion and Choice, Race, Racism, and Law," www. academic.udayton.edu/race, accessed September 29, 2009.

4. Michael Omi and Howard Winant, *Racial Formation in the United States: From the 1960s to the 1990s*, 2nd ed. (New York, NY: Routledge, 1994), 55.

5. Bennett deMarrais and LeCompte, *The Way Schools Work*, 289.

6. W. E. B. Du Bois, *The Souls of Black Folks*, Introduction by Herb Boyd (New York: Random House, The Modern Library, 1996), 15.

7. Cornel West, *Race Matters* (Boston, MA: Beacon Press, 1993), 3; W. E. B. Du Bois, *The Souls of Black Folks* (New York: Random House, The Modern Library, 1996), 15; John Hope Franklin, *The Color Line: Legacy for the Twenty-First Century* (Columbia, MO: University of Missouri Press, 1993), 5.

8. John Hope Franklin, "John Hope Franklin on Obama Nomination," Duke University News, http://www.youtube.com/watch?v= qPPNEpmcvIE, accessed October 14, 2009.

9. Barack Obama, "Barack Obama's Speech on Race," *New York Times,* www.nytimes.com/2008/03/18/us/politics/18text-obama.html, accessed October 10, 2009.

10. Gloria Steinem, *Revolution From Within: A Book of Self-Esteem* (New York: Simon & Schuster, 1992), 187.

11. Macon Phillips, "A Wonderful Day," The White House Blog, http://www.whitehouse.gov/blog_post/AWonderfulDay/, accessed October 10, 2009. As the president explains, Lilly Ledbetter worked "for nearly two decades before discovering that for years, she was paid less than her male colleagues for doing the very same work. Over the course of her career, she lost more than $200,000 in salary, and even more in pension and Social Security benefits—losses that she still feels today."

12. Maria Shriver, "The Shriver Report," a Study by Maria Shriver and the Center for American Progress, http://awomansnation.com, accessed October 20, 2009.

13. Gara La Marche, "Taking Account of Race: A Philanthropic Imperative," Waldemar Nielsen Issue Forums in Philanthropy, Georgetown University Center for Public and Nonprofit Leadership, Georgetown Public Policy Institute, http://atlanticphilanthropies.org/news, accessed October 18, 2009.

14. La Marche, "Taking Account of Race: A Philanthropic Imperative."

15. Emmett D. Carson, PhD, Forward, in Lynn Burbridge et al., "The Meaning and Impact of Board and Staff Diversity in the Philanthropic Field," Foreward by Emmett D. Carson, Joint Affinity Groups (Minneapolis, MN: The University of Minnesota, 2002), http://www.mcf.org/Mcf/resource/JAGreport.htm, accessed September 29, 2009, xvi.

16. Henry A. J. Ramos, Interview: Emmett D. Carson, PhD, Diversity in Philanthropy, http://www.diversityinphilanthropy.org/voices/interviews/, accessed September 20, 2009. Ramos indicates that Carson is an internally known leader in the field of philanthropy and charitable giving research.

17. La Marche, "Taking Account of Race: A Philanthropic Imperative."

18. Marla Cornelius, Patrick Corvington and Albert Ruesga, "Ready to Lead: Next Generation Leaders Speak Out" (Baltimore, MD:

CompassPoint Nonprofit Services, The Annie E. Casey Foundation & Meyer foundation, 2008), 16–20.

19. Mary Ellen S. Capek and Molly Mead, *Effective Philanthropy: Organizational Success through Deep Diversity and Gender Equality,* A Project of Women & Philanthropy funded by the W. K. Kellogg Foundation (Cambridge, MA: The MIT Press, 2006), 4.

20. Capek and Mead, *Effective Philanthropy,* 6–7. Capek and Mead use the term "deep diversity" to describe an "institutionalized understanding of diversity that goes *wide* as well as *deep.*" *Wide* consists of "gender, sexual orientation, gender identity, race, ethnicity, nationality, religion, class, disability," etc. The *deep* part includes "an organization's DNA" that goes into "the taproot of an organization and intertwined in the wide network of roots that anchors and feeds the whole of an organization's culture."

21. Camelia Suleiman and Daniel O'Connell, "Race and Gender in Current American Politics: A Discourse-Analytical Perspective," *Journal of Psycholinguistic Research,* 2008, vol. 37, no. 6, http://www.springerlink.com/content/9t1882175436m5lk/?p=93ba69e26b1d4fc198dc190ba5116169&pi=1, accessed September 23, 2009. In 2008, Suleiman and O'Connell conducted a study to examine the influence of race and gender on speech patterns. By watching interviews of Madeleine Albright, Bill Clinton, Hillary Clinton, Barack Obama, Colin Powell, and Condoleezza Rice, Suleiman and O'Connell concluded that there was a direct connection between race, gender, and speech.

22. Cornell West, *Race Matters* (Boston, MA: Beacon Press, 1993), 3.

23. Kenneth Cushner, Averil McClelland, and Philip Safford, *Human Diversity in Education: An Integrative Approach,* 2nd ed. (New York, NY: McGraw-Hill Companies, Inc., 1996), 65.

24. William E. Cross Jr., *Shades of Black: Diversity in African American Identity* (Philadelphia, PA: Temple University Press, 1991), as seen in Beverly Daniel Tatum, *Why Are All the Black Kids Sitting Together in the Cafeteria* (New York: Basic Books, 1997), 54.

25. Cross, *Shades of Black,* as seen in Tatum, *Why Are All the Black Kids Sitting Together in the Cafeteria,* 54, http://web.gc.cuny.edu/psychology/faculty/wcross.htm, accessed October 20, 2009. Also, see Beverly J. Vandiver, Peony E. Fhagen-Smith, Kevin O. Cokley, and William E. Cross Jr., "Cross's Nigrescence Model: From Theory to Scale to Theory," *Journal of Multicultural Counseling and*

Development, July 2001, vol. 29, no. 3, *ProQuest Psychology Journals,* 174–200.

26. Tatum, *Why Are All the Black Kids Sitting Together in the Cafeteria,* 54. Tatum has written numerous books examining race relations and identity, conducted workshops, facilitated forums, and taught psychology classes at several universities. Currently, she is the president of Spelman College.

27. Tatum, *Why Are All the Black Kids Sitting Together in the Cafeteria,* 55.

28. John Hope Franklin, *Mirror to America: The Autobiography of John Hope Franklin* (New York: Farrar, Straus and Giroux, 2005), 209–210.

29. Karen Kelley Ariwoola, interview.

30. Nancy Burd, interview.

31. Mary Catherine Bateson, *Composing a Life* (New York: PLUME, Penguin Books, 1990), 40.

32. Heather Arnet, interview.

33. Tatum, *Why Are All the Black Kids Sitting Together in the Cafeteria,* 55.

34. Tatum, *Why Are All the Black Kids Sitting Together in the Cafeteria,* 55.

35. Joseph L. Smith, interview.

36. Dwayne Ashley, interview.

37. "Living the Legacy: The Women's Rights Movement 1848–1998," History of the Movement, www.legacy98.org/move-hist. html, accessed October 10, 2009.

38. Heather Arnet, interview. Interestingly, while Orthodox Judaism's rules still strictly delineate gender roles throughout life—especially within a religious ritual context—in March 2009 the first Orthodox female rabbi was ordained and given the title Raba (a Hebrew acronym for a legal, spiritual, and Talmudic leader). Rabbi Avi Weiss of Riverdale, New York, bestowed the ordination on Raba Sara Hurwitz amid controversy within the larger Orthodox communities.

39. Tatum, *Why Are All the Black Kids Sitting Together in the Cafeteria,* 76.

40. Black families watched television shows such as *I Spy,* starring Bill Cosby; *Julia,* starring Dianne Carroll; and *Room 222,* starring Denise Nicholas.

41. Tatum, *Why Are All the Black Kids Sitting Together in the Cafeteria,* 82; Cushner et al., *Human Diversity in Education,* 65.

42. Cushner et al., *Human Diversity in Education*, 76.
43. Steinem, *Revolution from Within*, 66. Though Steinem used this term when discussing women's plight, it is nevertheless applicable for all these leaders. She posits that when persons are loved and lovable, valued and valuable just as they are, regardless of what they do, the most fundamental kind of self-esteem begins: "core" self-esteem.
44. Eduardo Bonilla-Silva, *Racism Without Racists* (Lanham, Maryland: Rowman Littlefield, 2003), 1.
45. Cushner et al., *Human Diversity in Education*, 76.
46. Phillip Thomas, interview.
47. Joseph L. Smith, interview.
48. Karen Kelley Ariwoola, interview.
49. Susan Taylor Batten, interview.
50. Phillip Thomas, interview.
51. Association of Black Foundation Executives, "Stepping Up and Stepping Out," edited by Marcus Littles, Ryan Bowers, and Micah Gilmers of Frontline Solutions, http://www.abfe.org/pdf/Stepping_Up_and_Stepping_Out.pdf, accessed October 1, 2009.

Chapter 3

1. Morris Price, interview.
2. Reatha Clark King, interview.
3. Joseph L. Smith Jr., interview.
4. Erica Hunt, interview.
5. Ibid., interview.
6. Mindy Lewis, interview.
7. Joseph L. Smith, interview.
8. Carol Goss, interview.
9. Phillip Thomas, interview.
10. Emmett Carson, interview.
11. Stephanie Greco Larson, *Media and Minorities: The Politics of Race in News and Entertainment* (Lanham, Maryland: Rowman & Littlefield, 2006), 24–36.
12. Janette L. Dates and William Barlow, *Split Image: African Americans in the Mass Media* (Washington, DC: Howard University Press, 1990), 253–261.
13. Ibid., 281.
14. Larson, *Media and Minorities*, 152.

15. Ibid., 153–157.
16. Marla Cornelius, Patrick Corvington, and Albert Ruesga, "Ready to Lead: Next Generation Leaders Speak Out" (Baltimore, MD: CompassPoint Nonprofit Services, The Annie E. Casey Foundation & Meyer foundation, 2008), 8.
17. Emmett Carson, interview.
18. Donna Hall, interview.
19. Lauren Casteel, interview.
20. Lisa Courtice, interview.
21. Tracy Souza, interview.
22. Erica Hunt, interview.
23. Carol Goss, interview.
24. Raymond D. Terrell and Randall B. Lindsey, *Culturally Proficient Leadership: The Personal Journey Begins Within* (California: Sage Publications, 2008).
25. Phillip Thomas, interview.
26. Heather Arnett, interview.
27. Ashton D. Trice and Linda Knapp, "Relationship of Children's Career Aspirations to Parent's Occupations," *Journal of Genetic Psychology* (September 1992), vol. 153, no. 3, 355–359.
28. Yvette Desrosiers-Alphonse, interview.
29. Jasmine Hall Ratlif, interview.
30. Denise McGregor Armbrister, interview.
31. Dwayne Ashley, interview.
32. Yvette Desrosiers-Alphonse, interview.
33. Nancy Burd, interview.
34. Reatha Clark King, interview.
35. Sarah Willie, "The College Experience of Black Students," *Black Scholar* (Fall 1995), vol. 25, no. 4, 70–74; Sarah Willie, *Acting Black: College, Identity, and the Performance of Race* (New York: Taylor & Francis, 2003).
36. Carol Goss, interview.
37. Johnetta B. Cole and Beverly Guy-Sheftal, *Gender Talk: The Struggle for Women's Equality in African American Communities* (New York: Random House, 2003); Patricia Hill Collins, *Black Feminist Thought: Knowledge, Consciousness, and the Politicas of Empowerment* (New York: Taylor & Francis, 1999). See also Marybeth Gasman, "Swept Under the Rug: A Historiography of Gender a Historically Black Colleges and Universities," *American Education Research Journal* (December 2007), vol. 44, no. 4, 760–805.

38. Emmett Carson, interview.
39. Ibid., interview.
40. Reatha Clark King, interview.
41. Ibid., interview.
42. Ibid., interview.
43. Heather Arnett, interview.
44. Tracey Souza, interview.
45. Carol Goss, interview.
46. Marybeth Gasman and Katherine V. Sedgwick (eds.), *Uplifting a People: African American Philanthropy and Education* (New York: Peter Lang, 2005). See also, Linda Stone (ed.), *New Directions in Anthropological Kinship* (Lanham: Rowman & Littlefield Publishers, 2001).
47. Bradford Smith, Sylvia Shue, Jennifer Lisa Vest, and Joseph Villarreal, *Philanthropy in Communities of Color* (Bloomington: Indiana University Press, 1999); Janice Gow Pettey, *Cultivating Diversity in Fundraising* (San Francisco: Wiley & Sons, 2002).
48. Lauren Casteel, interview.
49. Ibid., interview.
50. Emmett Carson, interview.
51. Richard J. Bentley and Luana G. Nissan, *The Roots of Giving and Serving* (Indianapolis: Indiana University Center on Philanthropy, 1996).
52. Paul G. Schervish and John J. Havens, "Social Participation and Charitable Giving: A Multivariate Analysis," *Voluntas: International Journal of Voluntary and Nonprofit Organizations* (1997), vol. 8, no. 3, 235–260. The 1992 Survey of Giving and Volunteering in the United States was collected by the Gallup Organization and the Independent Sector.
53. Morton M. Hunt, *The Compassionate Beast* (New York: William Morrow and Company, Inc., 1990).
54. Daniel Bar-Tal, *Prosocial Behavior: Theory and Research* (Washington, DC: Hemisphere Publishing Company, 1976); Richard J. Bentley and Luana G. Nissan, *The Roots of Giving and Serving* (Indianapolis: Indiana University Center on Philanthropy, 1996).
55. Gasman and Sedgwick, *Uplifting a People*.
56. Reatha Clark King, interview.
57. See Gasman and Sedgwick, *Uplifting a People*; and Marybeth Gasman and Sibby Anderson-Thompkins, *Fundraising from Black*

College Alumni: Successful Strategies for Supporting Alma Mater (Washington, DC: Council for the Advancement and Support of Education, 2003).

58. Joseph Smith, interview.
59. See Gasman and Sedgwick, *Uplifting a People*; and Gasman and Anderson-Thompkins, *Fundraising from Black College Alumni*.
60. Reatha Clark King, interview.
61. Phillip Thomas, interview.
62. Carol Goss, interview.
63. Dwayne Ashley, interview.
64. Susan Taylor Batten, interview.
65. Anonymous, interview.
66. Erica Hunt, interview. See also, David Garrow, "Philanthropy and the Civil Rights Movement," New York: Center for the Study of Philanthropy, Working Paper, CUNY Graduate Center, 1988.
67. Lauren Casteel, interview.
68. Mindy Lewis, interview.
69. See Gasman and Sedgwick, *Uplifting a People*; and Gasman and Anderson-Thompkins, *Fundraising from Black College Alumni*.

Chapter 4

1. Morris W. Price, interview.
2. Anonymous, interview.
3. Carol Goss, interview.
4. William Merritt, interview.
5. Reatha Clark King, interview.
6. Lauren Y. Casteel, interview.
7. Emmett Carson, interview.
8. Heather Arnet, interview.
9. Joseph L. Smith, interview.
10. William Merritt, interview.
11. Dwayne Ashley, interview.
12. Alicia Dixon, interview.
13. Ibid., interview.
14. Yvette Desrosiers-Alphonse, interview.
15. Erica Hunt, interview.
16. James Merritt, interview.

17. Emmett Carson, interview.
18. Carol Goss, interview.
19. Nancy Burd, interview.
20. Mindy McWilliams Lewis, interview.
21. Kassie Freeman and Gail E. Thomas, "Black Colleges and College Choice: Characteristics of Students Who Choose HBCUs," *The Review of Higher Education* (Spring 2002), vol. 25, no. 3, 349–358; Kassie Freeman, *African Americans and College Choice: The Influence of Family and School* (Albany, NY: State University of New York, 2005); Patricia McDonough, *Choosing Colleges: How Social Class and Schools Structure Opportunity* (Albany, NY: State University of New York, 1997).
22. Lauren Y. Casteel, interview.
23. Emmett Carson, interview.
24. Susan Taylor Batten, interview.
25. Marybeth Gasman, Valerie Lundy Wagner, Tafaya Ransom, and Nelson Bowman, *Unearthing Promise and Potential: Our Nation's Historically Black Colleges and Universities* (San Francisco: Jossey-Bass, 2010).
26. Phillip Thomas, interview.
27. Dwayne Ashley, interview.
28. Marybeth Gasman et al., *Unearthing Promise and Potential*; H. N. Drewry and H. Doermann, *Stand and Prosper: Private Black Colleges and Their Students* (Princeton, NJ: Princeton University Press, 2001); M. C. Brown and K. Freeman (eds.), *Black Colleges: New Perspectives on Policy and Practice* (Westport, CT: Praeger, 2004).
29. William E. Cross Jr., *Shades of Black: Diversity in African American Identity* (Philadelphia, PA: Temple University Press, 1991).
30. Kanyere Eaton, interview.
31. Ibid., interview.
32. Noah D. Drezner, "Cultivating a Culture of Giving: An Exploration of Institutional Strategies to Enhance African American Young Alumni Giving" (Ph.D. dissertation, University of Pennsylvania, 2008); Noah D. Drezner, "Why Give?: Exploring Social Exchange and Organizational Identification Theories in the Promotion of Philanthropic Behaviors of African American Millennials at Private-HBCUs," *International Journal of Educational Advancement* (Fall 2009), vol. 9, no. 3, 146–165; Noah D. Drezner, "Private Black Colleges' Encouragement of Student Giving and Volunteerism:

An Examination of Prosocial Behavior Development," *International Journal of Educational Advancement* (Winter 2010), vol. 10, no. 3, 126–147.

33. Ibid.; Marybeth Gasman, *Envisioning Black Colleges: A History of the United Negro College Fund* (Baltimore, MD: Johns Hopkins University Press, 2007).

34. Dwayne Ashley, interview.

35. Jasmine Ratcliff, interview.

36. Heather Arnett, interview.

37. Emmett Carson, interview.

38. Ibid., interview.

39. Ibid., interview.

40. William E. Cross Jr., *Shades of Black*.

Chapter 5

1. Merle Curti and Roderick Nash, *Philanthropy in the Shaping of American Higher Education* (New Brunswick, NJ: Rutgers University Press, 1965).

2. Gary A. Tobin, *The Transition of Communal Values and Behavior in Jewish Philanthropy* (San Francisco: Institute for Jewish & Community Research, 2001); Debra Susan Block, "Virtue Out of Necessity: A Study of Jewish Philanthropy in the United States, 1890–1918" (Ph.D. dissertation, University of Pennsylvania, 1997).

3. Linda Jones, "Christianity and Charity," *New Statesman* (2009). Retrieved electronically October 14, 2009, http://www.newstatesman.com/print/200904270002, n.p.

4. Ibid.

5. Emmett Carson, *Black Philanthropic Activity Past and Present: A 200 Year Tradition Continues* (Washington, DC: Joint Center for Political Studies, 1987); Emmett Carson, *Pulling Yourself Up by Your Bootstraps: The Evolution of Black Philanthropic Activity* (Washington, DC: Joint Center for Political Studies Press, 1987); Emmett Carson, *A Charitable Appeals Fact Book: How Black and White Americans Respond to Different Types of Fund-Raising Efforts* (Washington, DC: Joint Center for Political Studies Press, 1989); Emmett Carson, "Black Philanthropy: Shaping Tomorrow's Nonprofit Sector," *The National Society of Fund Raising Executives*

(NSFRE) Journal (Summer 1989), 23–31; Emmett Carson, *Black Volunteers as Givers and Fundraisers* (New York: Center for the Study of Philanthropy: City University of New York, 1990); Emmett Carson, "Patterns of Giving in Black Churches," in *Faith and Philanthropy in America: Exploring the Role of Religion in America's Voluntary Sector*, ed. Virginia A. Hodgkinson, Robert Wuthnow, and associates (San Francisco: Jossey-Bass Publishers, 1990); Emmett Carson, *A Hand Up: Black Philanthropy and Self-Help in America* (Washington, DC: Joint Center for Political Studies Press, 1993); Emmett Carson, "Giving Strength: Understanding Philanthropy in the Black Community," *Philanthropy Matters* (2001), vol. 2, no. 4, 2–4; Emmett Carson, "Black Philanthropy's Past, Present, and Future," *New Directions for Philanthropic Fundraising* (2005), vol. 48, 5–12; it should be noted that Carson is one of the foundation leaders interviewed for the Third Millennium Philanthropy and Leadership Initiative. Christopher G. Ellison and Darren L. Sherkat, "The 'Semi-involuntary Institution' Revisited: Regional Variations in Church Participation among Black Americans," *Social Forces* (1995), vol. 73, no. 4, 1415–1437; Noah D. Drezner, "The Black Church and Millennial Philanthropy: Influences on Student Giving," paper presented at Association for Research on Nonprofit Organizations and Voluntary Action Annual Meeting, Alexandria, VA, 2010.

6. Noah D. Drezner, "Cultivating a Culture of Giving: An Exploration of Institutional Strategies to Enhance African American Young Alumni Giving" (Ph.D. dissertation, University of Pennsylvania, 2008).

7. Robert H. Bremner, *Giving: Charity and Philanthropy in History* (New Brunswick: Transaction Publishers, 1996); Joan E. Grusec and Leon Kuczynski (ed.), *Parenting and Children's Internalization of Values: A Handbook of Contemporary Theory* (New York: Wiley, 1997); Richard Steinberg and Mark Wilhelm, "Giving: The Next Generation—Parental Effects on Donations" (Working Paper No. CPNS 21) (Indianapolis: Center on Philanthropy at Indiana University, 2003).

8. Drezner, "Cultivating a Culture of Giving"; Drezner, "The Black Church and Millennial Philanthropy: Influences on Student Giving."

9. Drezner, "Cultivating a Culture of Giving"; Bradford Smith, Sylvia Shue, Jennifer Lisa Vest, and Joseph Villarreal, *Philanthropy in*

Communities of Color (Bloomington, IN: Indiana University Press, 1999); Janice Gow Pettey, *Cultivating Diversity in Fundraising* (San Francisco, CA: Wiley & Sons, 2002).

10. Mark O. Wilhelm, Melissa Brown, Patrick M. Rooney, and Richard Steinberg, "The Intergenerational Transmission of Generosity," *Journal of Public Economics* (2008), vol. 92, no. 10–11, 2146.

11. Ibid., 2146, 2151.

12. Independent Sector, *Faith & Philanthropy: The Connection Between Charitable Behavior and Giving to Religion* (Washington, DC: Independent Sector, 2002).

13. Yvette Desrosiers-Alphonse, interview.

14. Ibid., interview.

15. Ibid., interview.

16. Ibid., interview.

17. Darryl B. Holloman, Marybeth Gasman and Sibby Anderson-Thompkins, "Motivations for Philanthropic Giving in the African American Church: Implications for Black College Fundraising," *Journal of Christian Education* (2003), vol. 12, 138.

18. Caprice Bragg, interview.

19. Morris Price, interview.

20. Daniel Bar-Tal, *Prosocial Behavior: Theory and Research* (Washington, DC: Hemisphere Publishing Company, 1976); Richard J. Bentley and Luana G. Nissan, *The Roots of Giving and Serving* (Indianapolis: Indiana University Center on Philanthropy, 1996).

21. Reatha Clark King, interview.

22. Bar-Tal, *Prosocial Behavior*; Bentley and Nissan, *The Roots of Giving and Serving*.

23. Anita H. Plotinsky, "From Generation to Generation: Transmitting the Jewish Philanthropic Tradition," *New Directions for Philanthropic Fundraising: Cultures of Giving: How Region and Religion Influence Philanthropy* (1995), vol. 7, 117–132.

24. Heather Arnet, interview.

25. Ibid., interview.

26. Nancy Burd, interview.

27. David L. Rosenhan, "The Natural Socialization of Altruistic Autonomy," in *Altruism and Help Behavior*, ed. J. Macauley and L. Berkowitz (New York: Academic Press, 1970), 251–268.

28. Gregory L. Cascione, *Philanthropists in Higher Education: Institutional, Biographical, and Religious Motivations for Giving* (New York: Routledge Falmer, 2003).

29. Ibid.
30. Holloman, Gasman & Anderson-Thompkins, "Motivations for Philanthropic Giving in the African American Church: Implications for Black College Fundraising," 146.
31. Mindy McWilliams Lewis, interview.
32. David L. Rosenhan, "The Natural Socialization of Altruistic Autonomy," in *Altruism and Help Behavior*, ed. J. Macauley and L. Berkowitz (New York: Academic Press, 1970), 251–268; Gregory L. Cascione, *Philanthropists in Higher Education: Institutional, Biographical, and Religious Motivations for Giving* (New York: Routledge Falmer, 2003).
33. Morris Price, interview.
34. Ibid., interview.
35. Holloman, Gasman & Anderson-Thompkins, 148–152.
36. Christopher G. Ellison and Darren L. Sherkat, 'The "Semi-involuntary Institution' Revisited: Regional Variations in Church Participation among Black Americans," *Social Forces* (1995), vol. 73, no. 4, 1415.
37. For example, Emmett Carson, *Black Philanthropic Activity Past and Present: A 200 Year Tradition Continues* (Washington, DC: Joint Center for Political Studies, 1987); Emmett Carson, *Pulling Yourself Up by Your Bootstraps: The Evolution of Black Philanthropic Activity* (Washington, DC: Joint Center for Political Studies Press, 1987); Emmett Carson, *A Charitable Appeals Fact Book: How Black and White Americans Respond to Different Types of Fund-Raising Efforts* (Washington, DC: Joint Center for Political Studies Press, 1989); Emmett Carson, "Black Philanthropy: Shaping Tomorrow's Nonprofit Sector," *The National Society of Fund Raising Executives (NSFRE) Journal* (1989, Summer), 23–31; Emmett Carson, *Black Volunteers as Givers and Fundraisers* (New York: Center for the Study of Philanthropy: City University of New York, 1990); Emmett Carson, "Patterns of Giving in Black Churches," in *Faith and Philanthropy in America: Exploring the Role of Religion in America's Voluntary Sector*, ed. Virginia A. Hodgkinson, Robert Wuthnow, and associates (San Francisco: Jossey-Bass Publishers, 1990); Emmett Carson, *A Hand Up: Black Philanthropy and Self-Help in America* (Washington, DC: Joint Center for Political Studies Press, 1993); Emmett Carson, "Giving Strength: Understanding Philanthropy in the Black Community," *Philanthropy Matters* (2001), vol. 2, no. 4, 2–4; Emmett Carson, "Black Philanthropy's Past, Present,

and Future," *New Directions for Philanthropic Fundraising* (2005), vol. 48, 5–12; it should be noted that Carson is one of the foundation leaders interviewed for the Third Millennium Philanthropy and Leadership Initiative. Christopher G. Ellison and Darren L. Sherkat, "The 'Semi-involuntary Institution' Revisited: Regional Variations in Church Participation among Black Americans," *Social Forces* (1995), vol. 73, no. 4 1415–1437; Virginia A. Hodgkinson and Murray S. Weitzman, *Giving and Volunteering in the United States: Findings from a National Survey* (Washington, DC: Independent Sector, 1996); Christopher G. Ellison and Darren L. Sherkat, "The 'Semi-involuntary Institution' Revisited: Regional Variations in Church Participation among Black Americans," *Social Forces* (1995), vol. 73, no. 4 1415–1437; Mark O. Wilhelm, Melissa Brown, Patrick M. Rooney, and Richard Steinberg, "The Intergenerational Transmission of Generosity," *Journal of Public Economics* (2008), vol. 92, no. 10–11, 2146–2156.

38. Harold Dean Trulear, "Philanthropy and religion," in Rodney M. Jackson (ed.), *A Philanthropic Covenant with Black America* (Hoboken: John Wiley & Sons, 2009), 30–31.

39. Kanyere Eaton, interview.

40. Ibid., interview.

41. Ibid., interview.

42. Christopher G. Ellison and Darren L. Sherkat, "The 'Semi-involuntary Institution' Revisited: Regional Variations in Church Participation among Black Americans," *Social Forces* (1995), vol. 73, no. 4, 1415–1437; Norval D. Glenn, "Negro Religion and Negro Status in the United States," in *Religion, Culture, and Society*, ed. Louis Schneider (New York: Wiley,1964), 623–629; Cardell K. Jacobson, Tim B. Heaton and Rutledge M. Dennis, "Black-White Differences in Religiosity: Item Analyses and a Formal Structural Test," *Sociological Analysis* (1990), vol. 51, no. 3, 257–270; Wade Clark Roof and William McKinney, *American Mainline Religion* (New Brunswick, NJ: Rutgers University Press, 1987).

43. Ellison and Sherkat, "The 'Semi-involuntary Institution' Revisited: Regional Variations in Church Participation Among Black Americans," 1415–1437.

44. Lauren Casteel, interview.

45. Ibid., interview.

Chapter 6

1. Interviews with Joseph L. Smith Sr., Tracy Souza, Kanyere Eaton, Heather Arnet, Dwayne Ashley, and Susan Taylor Batten.
2. Phillip Thomas, interview.
3. Caprice Bragg, interview.
4. Denise McGregor Armbrister, interview.
5. Cornelius, Corvington & Ruesga, 4.
6. Ibid.
7. Ibid., 16.
8. Ibid., 3.
9. William Merritt, interview.
10. Reatha Clark King, interview.
11. William Merritt, interview.
12. Ibid., interview.
13. Marla Cornelius, Patrick Corvington, and Albert Ruesga, "Ready to Lead? Next Generation Leaders Speak Out" (Washington, DC: CompassPoint Nonprofit Services, The Annie E. Casey Foundation, the Meyer Foundation, and Idealist.org, 2008), 3.
14. Emmett Carson, interview.
15. Karen Kelley Ariwoola, interview.
16. Cornelius, Corvington & Ruesga, 10.
17. Karen Kelley Ariwoola, interview.
18. Ibid.
19. Ibid.
20. "Ready to Lead? Next Generation Leaders Speak Out." By Marla Cornelius, Patrick Corvington, and Albert Ruesga. Washington, DC: CompassPoint Nonprofit Services, The Annie E. Casey Foundation, the Meyer Foundation, and Idealist.org, 2008. 3.
21. Kanyere Eaton, interview.
22. Karen Kelley Ariwoola, interview.
23. Ibid.
24. Ibid.
25. Cornelius, Corvington & Ruesga, 24.
26. "Ready to Lead? Next Generation Leaders Speak Out." By Marla Cornelius, Patrick Corvington, and Albert Ruesga. Washington, DC: CompassPoint Nonprofit Services, The Annie E. Casey Foundation, the Meyer Foundation, and Idealist.org, 2008, 18.
27. Jeanne Bell, Richard Moyers and Timothy Wolfred, "Daring to Lead 2006: A National Study of Nonprofit Executive Leadership"

(Washington, DC: CompassPoint Nonprofit Services & the Meyer Foundation, 2006), 3.

28. Susan Taylor Batten, interview.
29. Willis K. Bright, interview.
30. "Ready to Lead? Next Generation Leaders Speak Out," 8.
31. Ibid.
32. Ibid.
33. Emmett Carson, interview.
34. Kanyere Eaton, interview.

Chapter 7

1. Anonymous leader, interview.

Supplementary Bibliography

Abbe, M. A. (2000). The roots of minority giving. *Currents, 26*(6), 36–40.

Adetimirin, A. (2008). Crisis in Black nonprofits. *Network Journal, 15*(9), 10.

Aguirre, A., & Min, L. (2005). *Familia, fé y comunidad: Giving and Volunteering among Hispanics in Silicon Valley.* San Jose, CA: Community Foundation Silicon Valley.

Anderson, B. E. (1993). *Philanthropy and Charitable Giving among Large Black Business Owners.* Indianapolis, IN: Association of Black Foundation Executives.

Anft, M. (2007, October 18). Inching to the top: Nonprofit managers who are minorities search for a quicker way up the ladder. *The Chronicle of Philanthropy, 20*(1), 4.

Anonymous. (2001). New coalition promotes ethnic philanthropy in New York. *The CPA Journal, 71*(12), 18.

Arca, P. (1994). Why diversity? *Advancing Philanthropy, 2*, 11–13.

Asian American Federation. (2001). *A New Heritage of Giving: Philanthropy in Asian America.* New York: Asian American Federation of New York.

Asian Pacific American Community Fund. (1996). Asian *Pacific American Nonprofits: Perceptions and Realities.* San Francisco, CA: Asian Pacific American Community Fund.

Asimov, N. (1990, June 25). White males dominate foundation boards: Watchdog group surveyed 75 boards across U.S.—5 in Bay Area. *San Francisco Chronicle,* pp. A5.

Baron, B., & Bozorgmehr, M. (2001). *Philanthropy among Middle Eastern Americans and Their Historical Traditions of Giving.* New York: Center for the Study of Philanthropy, City University of New York.

Bartlett, C. V. (2003, December 16). Beyond numbers and compliance: Valuing cultural diversity in national nonprofit capacity-building organizations. *ENHANCE: The Newsletter of the Alliance for Nonprofit Management, 1,* 1–10.

Bartolini, W. F. (2001). Using a communication perspective to manage diversity in the development office. *New Directions for Philanthropic Fundraising, 34,* 47–75.

Baugh, L. L. (Ed). (2005). Black philanthropy: From words to action. *Proceedings of the Fourth National Conference on Black Philanthropy.* Washington, DC: National Center for Black Philanthropy.

Berkshire, J. C. (2008, September 18). Missing persons: Why do so few Black men hold top leadership jobs at nonprofit groups? *The Chronicle of Philanthropy, 20*(23), 8–10.

Berry, M. L., & Chao, J. (2001). *Engaging Diverse Communities for and through Philanthropy.* Washington, DC: Forum of Regional Associations of Grantmakers.

Billitteri, T. J., Blum, D. E., Lipman, H., Marchetti, D., Moore, J., Sommerfeld, M., Williams, G., & Voelz, M. (1999, September 23). Top leaders see fatter paychecks. *The Chronicle of Philanthropy, 11,* 35–49.

Bordas, J. (2007). *Salsa, Soul, and Spirit: Leadership for a Multicultural Age.* San Francisco, CA: Berrett-Koehler Publications.

Boyers, K. (1995). Thinking about diversity: Five association executives discuss the value of difference. *Association Management, 47*(6), 42–45, 47, 68.

Brown, W. A. (2002). Inclusive governance practices in nonprofit organizations and implications for practice. *Nonprofit Management & Leadership, 12*(4), 369–385.

Bryson, E., & Parsons, S. (2003). *What Foundation Boards are Saying about Diversity?* Washington, DC: Council on Foundations.

Burbridge, L. C. (1995). *Status of African Americans in Grant Making Institutions.* Indianapolis, IN: Indiana University Center on Philanthropy.

Burbridge, L. C., Diaz, W. A., Odendahl, T., & Shaw, A. (2002). *The Meaning and Impact of Board and Staff Diversity in the Philanthropic Field: Findings from a National Study.* San Francisco, CA: Joint Affinity Groups.

Byrd, A. (Ed.). (1990). *Philanthropy and the Black Church.* Washington, DC: Council on Foundations.

Campoamor, D., Diaz, W. A., & Ramos, H. A. J. (Eds.). (1999). *Nuevos Senderos: Reflections on Hispanics and Philanthropy.* Houston, TX: Arte Publico Press.

Capek, M. E. S., & Mead, M. (2006). *Effective Philanthropy: Organizational Success through Deep Diversity and Gender Equality.* Cambridge: MIT Press.

Carson, E. D. (1994). Diversity and equity among foundation grant makers. *Nonprofit Management and Leadership, 4*(3), 331–344.

Carson, E. D. (2005). Black philanthropy's past, present and future. *New Directions for Philanthropic Fundraising, 48,* 5–12.

Carver, J., & Carver, M. M. (1997). *Making Diversity Meaningful in the Boardroom.* San Francisco, CA: Jossey-Bass.

Center for Nonprofit Management of the Graduate School of Business. (1995). *Dialogue on Diversity (Part 1).* St. Thomas, Virgin Islands: University of St. Thomas.

Chandler, L. C. (2005). Beyond political correctness: Discover the benefits of board diversity. *Association Management, 57*(1), 29–30.

Chao, J. (2001). Asian-American philanthropy: Acculturation and charitable vehicles. *ARNOVA, 1*(1), 57–79.

Clift, E. (Ed.). (2005). *Women, Philanthropy and Social Change.* Medford, MA: Tufts University Press.

Clohesy, S. J. (2004). *Donor Circles: Launching and Leveraging Shared Giving.* San Francisco, CA: Women's Funding Network.

Conley, D. (2000). The racial wealth gap: Origins and implications for philanthropy in the African American community. *Nonprofit and Voluntary Sector Quarterly, 29*(4), 530.

Cornelius, M., & Lew, S. (2009). What about the next generation of leaders of color? Advancing multicultural leadership. *Nonprofit World, 27*(4), 24–26.

Cortés, M. (1999). Do Hispanic nonprofits foster Hispanic philanthropy? *New Directions for Philanthropic Fundraising, 24,* 31–24.

Council on Foundations. (1993). *Inclusive Practices in Philanthropy: Report and Commentary of the Council on Foundations Task Force on Inclusiveness and Staff.* Washington, DC: Council on Foundations.

Council on Foundations. (1999). *Cultures of Caring: Philanthropy in Diverse American Communities.* Washington, DC: Council on Foundations.

Daley, J. M. (2002). An action guide for nonprofit board diversity. *Journal of Community Practice, 10*(1), 33–54.

Delgado, L. T., Orellana-Damacela, L. E., & Zanoni, M. J. (2001). *Chicago Philanthropy: A Profile of the Grant Making Profession.* Chicago, IL: Loyola University Chicago.

Enay, S. (2009). Big island: GIRL POWER. *Hawaii Business, 54*(8), 18.

Ewin, A., & Wollock, J. (1996). *Survey of Grant Giving by American Indian Foundations and Organizations.* Lumberton, NC: Native Americans in Philanthropy.

Expanding Nonprofit Inclusiveness Initiative. (2003). *Inside Inclusiveness: Race, Ethnicity and Nonprofit Organizations.* Denver, CO: The Denver Foundation.

Fairfax, J. E. (1995). Black philanthropy: Its heritage and its future. *New Directions for Philanthropic Fundraising, 6,* 9–21.

Fletcher, K. (1997). *Building Board Diversity: A Case Study of the Western Affiliates of Planned Parenthood Federation of America.* Queenstown, MD: The Aspen Institute.

Friedman, L. J., & McGarvie, M. D. (Eds.). (2003). *Charity, Philanthropy, and Civility in American History.* Bloomington, MN: Indiana University Press.

Gallegos, H. E., & O'Neill, M. (Eds.). (1991). *Hispanics and the Nonprofit Sector.* New York: Foundation Center.

Gardyn, R. (2003, December 11). Building board diversity. *The Chronicle of Philanthropy, 16*(5), 25–26.

Gary, T., & Kohner, M. (2002). *Inspired Philanthropy: Creating a Giving Plan.* Berkeley, CA: Chardon Press.

Ginsberg, L. D. (1990). *Women and the Work of Benevolence: Morality, Politics, and Class in the Nineteenth Century United States.* New Haven, CT: Yale University Press.

Gitin, M. (2001). Beyond representation: Building diverse board leadership teams. *New Directions for Philanthropic Fundraising, 34,* 77–100.

Greene, M. P. (2007). Beyond diversity and multiculturalism: Towards the development of anti-racist institutions and leaders. *Journal for Nonprofit Management, 11,* 9–17.

Greene, S. G., Hall, H., & Stehle, V. (1994, September 20). The nonprofit world's diversity dilemma. *The Chronicle of Philanthropy, 6,* 26–29.

Gurevitz, S. (1994). The long march. *NonProfit Times, 8,* 1, 17–9.

Gutiérrez, J. A. (n.d.). *Report on Latinos and Philanthropy in the United States.* New York: Center on Philanthropy and Civil Society, City University of New York.

Hall, H. (1999, June 3). Black philanthropy: A focus on careers and building endowments. *The Chronicle of Philanthropy, 11*, 31–32.

Hallgarth, S., & Capek, M. E. (1995). *Who Benefits, Who Decides? An Agenda for Improving Philanthropy: The Case for Women and Girls*. New York: National Council for Research on Women.

Hall-Russell, C., & Kasberg, R. H. (1997). *African American Traditions of Giving and Serving: A Midwest Perspective*. Indianapolis, IN: Indiana University Center on Philanthropy.

Hamilton, C. H., & Ilchman, W. R. (1995). *Cultures of Giving II: How Heritage, Gender, Wealth and Values Influence Philanthropy*. San Francisco, CA: Jossey-Bass.

Harris, A. S. (1994). Blacks still face barriers at nonprofits. *NonProfit Times, 8*(1), 14–15.

Hesselbein, F., & Goldsmith, M. (Eds.). (2006). *The Leader of the Future 2: Visions, Strategies, and Practices for the Next Era*. San Francisco, CA: Jossey-Bass.

Hine, D. C. (1994). *Hine Sight: Black Women and the Reconstruction of American History*. Bloomington, MN: Indiana University Press.

Hispanics in Philanthropy. (2004). *Reflection, Action, and Expansion: Analysis of the Challenges and Opportunities for the Development of Emerging Latino Community in Boulder County, Colorado*. San Francisco, CA: Hispanics in Philanthropy.

Hunt, E. (2003). *African-American Philanthropy: A Legacy of Giving*. New York: Twenty-First Century Foundation.

Hunt, E., & Maurrasse, D. (2004). *Time, Talent and Treasure: A Study of Black Philanthropy*. New York: Twenty-First Century Foundation.

Jackson, R. M. (Ed.). (1998). At the crossroads. *Proceedings of the First National Conference on Black Philanthropy*. Oakton, VA: The Corporation for Philanthropy.

Jackson, R. M. (Ed.). (2000a). Moving the agenda forward. *Proceedings of the Second National Conference on Black Philanthropy*. Washington, DC: National Center for Black Philanthropy.

Jackson, R. M. (Ed.). (2000b). *Philanthropy and the Black Church: New Problems/New Visions*. Vienna, VA: Corporation for Philanthropy.

Jackson, T. D. (2001). Young African Americans: A new generation of giving behavior. *International Journal of Nonprofit and Voluntary Sector Marketing, 6*(3), 243.

Joseph, J. A. (1995). *Remaking America: How the Benevolent Traditions of Many Cultures are Transforming Our National Life*. San Francisco, CA: Jossey-Bass.

Joslyn, H. (2007, October 18). Image vs. reality: The nonprofit's world of inclusion is still a dream for many organizations. *The Chronicle of Philanthropy, 20*(1), 3.

Joslyn, H. (2009, September 17). A man's world. *The Chronicle of Philanthropy, 21*(21), 39.

Kaminski, A. R. (2003). Women as donors. In H. A. Rosso and E. R. Tempel (Eds.), *Achieving Excellence in Fund Raising* (pp. 200–214). San Francisco, CA: Jossey-Bass.

Kasper, G., Ramos, H. A. J., & Walker, C. J. (2004). Making the case for diversity in philanthropy. *Foundation News & Commentary, 45*(6), 26–35.

Lee, R. (1990). *Guide to Chinese American Philanthropy and Charitable Giving Patterns*. San Rafael, CA: Pathway Press.

Light, I., Kwuon, I. J., & Zhong, D. (1990). Korean rotating credit associations in Los Angeles. *Amerasia, 16*(1), 35–54.

Lindsey, K. R. (2006). *Racial, Ethnic, and Tribal hilanthropy: A Scan of the Landscape*. Washington, DC: Forum of Regional Associations of Grantmakers.

Lipman, H. (2002). Minority homeowners give more to charity than Whites, study finds. *The Chronicle of Philanthropy, 14*(6), 14.

McKinley-Floyd, L. A. (1998). The impact of values on the selection of philanthropic clubs by elite African American women: An historical perspective. *Psychology & Marketing, 15*(2), 145.

McCarthy, K. D. (Ed.). (1990). *Lady Bountiful Revisited: Women, Philanthropy and Power*. New Brunswick, NJ: Rutgers University Press.

Miller, J. L., Fletcher, K., & Abzug, R. (1999). *Perspectives on Nonprofit Board Diversity*. Washington, DC: National Center for Nonprofit Boards.

Minnesota Council on Foundations. (2005). *Working Towards Diversity III: A Progress Report on Strategies for Inclusiveness among Minnesota Grant Makers*. Minneapolis, MN: Minnesota Council on Foundations.

Moore, J. (1993, November 16). Nonprofits trail government and business in ethnic and racial diversity. *The Chronicle of Philanthropy, 6*, 27–30.

Morrison, A. M. (1992). *The New Leaders: Guidelines on Leadership Diversity in America*. San Francisco, CA: Jossey-Bass.

Mottino, F., & Miller, E. D. (2004). *Pathways for Change: Philanthropy among African American, Asian American and Latino Donors in the*

New York Metropolitan Region. New York: Center on Philanthropy and Civil Society at the City University of New York.

National Committee for Responsible Philanthropy. (2004). *State of Philanthropy 2004.* Washington, DC: National Committee for Responsible Philanthropy.

Newman, D. (2002). *Opening Doors: Pathways to Diverse Donors.* San Francisco, CA: Jossey-Bass.

Ostrower, F. (2007). *Nonprofit Governance in the United States: Findings on Performance and Accountability from the First National Representative Study.* Washington, DC: The Urban Institute.

Paupard, J. (1995). *American Indians and Philanthropy: A Summary Report of the December 1994 Forum.* St. Paul, MN: American Indian Research and Policy Institute.

Perry, S. (2006, September 28). Tapping Hispanic philanthropy. *The Chronicle of Philanthropy, 18*(24), 7–12.

Ramos, H. A. J., & Kasper, G. (2000). *Building a Tradition of Latino Philanthropy: Hispanics as Donors, Grantees, Grant Makers, and Volunteers.* Los Angeles: Center on Philanthropy and Public Policy, University of Southern California.

Rogers, P. C. (1999). African American traditions of giving and serving: A Midwest perspective. *Nonprofit and Voluntary Sector Quarterly, 28*(3), 348.

Rogers, P. C. (Ed.). (2001). *Philanthropy in Communities of Color: Traditions and Challenges.* Indianapolis, IN: Association for Research on Nonprofit Organizations and Voluntary Action.

Romero, A. D. (1998). *Globalized Latinos: The Opportunities and Challenges of Leadership—An Address to the Hispanics in Philanthropy Board of Directors.* Santo Domingo, Dominican Republic: Hispanics in Philanthropy.

Royce, A. P., & Rodriguez, R. (1999). From personal charity to organized giving: Hispanic institutions and values of stewardship and philanthropy. *New Directions for Philanthropic Fundraising, 24,* 9–29.

Rutledge, J. M. (1994). *Building Board Diversity.* Washington, DC: National Center for Nonprofit Boards.

Rutnik, T. A., & Bearman, J. (2005). *Giving Together: A National Scan of Giving Circles and Shared Giving.* Washington, DC: Forum of Regional Associations of Grantmakers.

Samuels, D. (1995, September 18). Philanthropic correctness: The failure of American foundations. *The New Republic, 213*(12/13), 28–36.

Schneider, J. A. (2003). Small, minority-based nonprofits in the information age. *Nonprofit Management & Leadership, 13*(4), 383.

Shaw, S. C., & Taylor, M. A. (1995). *Reinventing Fundraising: Realizing the Potential of Women's Philanthropy.* San Francisco, CA: Jossey-Bass.

Shaw-Hardy, S. (2000). *Creating a Women's Giving Circle.* Rochester, MI: Women's Philanthropy Institute.

Shrestha, N., McKinley-Floyd, L., & Gillespie, M. (2008). Promoting philanthropy in the Black community: A macroscopic exploration. *Journal of Macromarketing, 28*(1), 91.

Sidberry, T. B. (2002). Building diversity in organizations. *Nonprofit Quarterly, 8*(2), 28–33.

Siska, D. (2000). Getting to know you. *Foundation News & Commentary, 41*(1), 27.

Smith, B., Shue, S., Vest, J. L., & Villarreal, J. (1999). *Philanthropy in Communities of Color.* Bloomington, MN: Indiana University Press.

Smith, B., Shue, S., & Villarreal, J. (1999). *Asian and Hispanic Philanthropy.* San Francisco, CA: Institute for Nonprofit Organization Management.

Souccar, M. K. (2002, May 27). Lunching ladies meet hip-hop: A charity finds new donors, vitality. *Crain's New York Business, 18*(21), 3–4.

Soutar, S. (2004). Beyond the rainbow: Infusing your organization with diversity know-how. *Association Management, 56*(4), 26–31.

Spann, J., & Springer, C. (1993). *The Value of Difference: Enhancing Philanthropy through Inclusiveness in Governance, Staffing and Grant Making.* Washington, DC: Council on Foundations.

Taylor, M. A., & Shaw-Hardy, S. (Eds.). (2005). *The Transformative Power of Women's Philanthropy: New Directions for Philanthropic Fundraising, No. 50.* San Francisco, CA: Jossey-Bass.

Teltsch, K., & Joseph, J. A. (1990, April 7). At foundations, the voice of women and minorities remains faint. *The New York Times*, p. 9.

Tempel, E. R., & Smith, L. (2007, March 1). Leadership diversity: The nonprofit sector has a spotty record on advancement. *NonProfit Times, 21*(5), 14–15.

Van Slyke, D. M., Ashley, S., & Johnson, J. L. (2007). Nonprofit performance, fund-raising effectiveness, and strategies for engaging African Americans in philanthropy. *American Review of Public Administration, 37*(3), 278.

Von Schlegell, A. J., & Fisher, J. M. (1993). *Women as Donors, Women as Philanthropists.* San Francisco, CA: Jossey-Bass.

Wagner, L., & Patrick, R. J. (2004). Achieving diversity among fundraising professionals. *New Directions for Philanthropic Fundraising, 43,* 63–70.

Walton, A. (Ed.). (2005). *Women and Philanthropy in Education.* Bloomington,MN: Indiana University Press.

Welankiwar, R. (2009). CARE CEO Helene Gayle on shaking up a venerable organization. *Harvard Business Review, 87*(4), 22.

Winters, M. F. (1996). *Include me! Making the Case for Inclusiveness for Private and Family Foundations.* Washington, DC: Council on Foundations.W. K. Kellogg Foundation. (1999). *Emerging Philanthropy in Communities of Color: A Report on Current Trends.* Battle Creek, MI: W. K. Kellogg Foundation.

Women and Foundations/Corporate Philanthropy. (1990). *Far from Done: The Challenge of Diversifying Philanthropic Leadership.* New York: Women and Foundations/Corporate Philanthropy.

Index